# Parenting against the tide

—a handbook for twenty-first century
Christian parents

Ann Benton

**EP BOOKS**
Faverdale North
Darlington
DL3 0PH, England

web: http://www.epbooks.org

e-mail: sales@epbooks.org

EP Books are distributed in the USA by:
JPL Distribution
3741 Linden Avenue Southeast
Grand Rapids, MI 49548
E-mail: orders@jpldistribution.com
Tel: 877.683.6935

**British Library Cataloguing in Publication Data available**

ISBN: 978-1-78397-035-3

Printed by Bell and Bain Ltd, Glasgow

This book is dedicated with love to

Matt and Chrisi

Tom and Rebecca

Jess and Pete

Owen and Missy

who already know what it is to swim against the tide.

Keep going.

There are many books on parenting by self-appointed experts who give us a bucketful of sugar to help the medicine go down. Ann Benton's parenting book is different. It is full of not just home truths but biblical truths. It is a handbook in the mode of a manual helping parents to work through what it means to be biblical parents and what to watch out for along the way.

Ann does not pull her punches. She puts the spotlight on an age which seeks pleasure first; on parenting which dances to the tune of the recent hit song 'Happy' with the catchy lyrics 'clap along if you think happiness is the truth'.

Ann is deliberately and faithfully going against the tide of a worldview about parenting. Some will find it uncomfortable and hard hitting but most will recognise the loving desire to reveal God's truth about parenting.

The book is designed to be helpful and it ends each chapter with 'practical inferences and applications' and further reading. It is a serious book to be read and worked through, which will probably not leave you entertained but will leave you challenged and encouraged. Ann reminds us that the Bible has all the answers and the model for parenting. She describes the Bible worldview of a child worthy of the utmost respect—not a product of chance but made in the image of God; a child born into a system of care built around the Commandment to 'Honour your father and mother so that you may live long in the land'.

The central message of Ann's book and indeed the Bible to parents is that it is in the best interests of a child to be under his parents' authority, obedient to them. The book does not take parents on a guilt trip, nor does it smother them with false comfort. Amidst a plethora of advice and tips from 'experts', the great and often not so good, biblical parenting gives in Ann's words 'simplicity, liberty and joy to raising children'. It provides parents who believe the Bible with the confidence to be parents as God intended and as he modelled.

By writing this book and, somewhat reluctantly publishing it, Ann has done a service for us all by putting firmly down on paper the standard of God's infallible word against the secularist tide which washes into our family life. It is a gritty, real, honest and above all truthful book which points us to the best parent of all—Our Father God.

**David Burrowes MP**

Ann Benton's *Parenting Against the Tide* is simply superb. Here is a book that equips Christian parents to be careful, wise, and God-honoring in doing what is best both for their children and for their homes, more broadly. This book is based on Biblical principles and it provides also clear application of these principles. It contains much common (actually, not so common) sense which parents will find so very helpful. The book demonstrates clearly how to raise a family based on the foundation of the true, inspired, and inerrant Word of God. Additionally, it gives clear guidance on maintaining the primacy of the marriage relationship, which is so refreshing in this day of child-centered parenting. This well-written, inspiring, practical, and winsome book will help parents sort through the muddled confusion they face. We highly recommend this parenting book, one of the best we have read.

**Bruce and Jodi Ware**
The Southern Baptist Theological Seminary, Louisville, Kentucky, USA

This book brilliantly punctures many of the current orthodoxies surrounding children and parenting. Ann Benton shows that as we set out to please God in fulfilling our role as parents, that is the surest road to joy in family life. Each chapter is full of biblical wisdom and common sense.

**Dr Sharon James, author and conference speaker.**

# Contents

Acknowledgements     9

Introduction: Another book on parenting?     11
  *Some things are much harder than they used to be*

1. Mother knows best (and Father too)     17
  *A discussion of parenthood and parental authority*

2. The myth of self-esteem     33
  *How an urban myth turned parenting upside down
  and made us afraid of our children*

3. Right and Wrong—who says so?     50
  *The muddle created by relativism*

4. Delighting in our children     63
  *As our heavenly Father delights in us*

5. The wonderful concept of obedience     82
  *Biblical parenting is both simple and beautiful*

6. The rod of correction     99
  *Is the naughty step all we need?*

7. Manly boys and feminine girls     112
  *Gender distinctives without stereotyping*

8. Sex and the Christian family 129
 *Countering the secular lies about love, sex and marriage*
9. Net gain or net loss 147
 *Children and communications technology*
10. Spend, spend, spend 161
 *The perils of living in an affluent society*
11. Is it indoctrination? 179
 *Fearlessly passing on the baton of truth*
12. Can we trust our children to others? 196
 *Home-schooling and its alternatives*
13. Sunday blessings or Sunday blues 209
 *Children and church*
14. Aims and ambitions 225
 *What do we want for our children?*
Conclusion 237
 *'I can't do this.'*

# Acknowledgements

Many different people have contributed to this book and most of them did so quite unconsciously. I am indebted to the many parents I have conversed with up and down the country, the faithful Bible teachers who have opened up the Scriptures and the numerous writers I have read on and around the various issues I tackle. It is not impossible that a few of them may find themselves roughly quoted without attribution. I have not in every case been able to recall the source. I apologise.

But I want to particularly thank Steve Pannifer, Stefan Cantore, Roger Loosley and Nick and Rachael Healey who gave me both their time and the benefit of their expertise in areas where I was ignorant.

I would also like to acknowledge the contribution of some of the people who read an earlier incarnation of this book. Their feedback was not kind but it was on some points just. I valued the insights of those readers and used them to make adjustments, plug gaps and write what I hope is a better book. However, on very careful and serious consideration I found some of their comments to reveal a stance somewhat adrift from Scripture. In so far as they recognised a tide they thought it a benign tide and saw little reason to stand against it. This also was helpful because it underlined to me the very necessity for this book. On both counts I am grateful to those readers. I bear them no ill-will.

This book has not been easy to write. It came a twitching finger away from being deleted. At best it would have lain forgotten in a drawer had it not been for four people.

So, sincere and heartfelt gratitude to: Margaret Rush, my faithful driver and minder, who has patiently listened and prayed; Esther Matthews, who encouraged me at a particularly low point; Sharon James, who quite unwittingly spurred me on to get the manuscript out and finish the job.

Most of all I want to thank my brilliant husband John. His book, 'Christians in a PC world', was my starting point. His wisdom and vast knowledge about all kinds of things informed the many discussions we have had, piecemeal, at the table, in the car and walking on the Surrey Downs over the last couple of years. He has also patiently and painstakingly read every chapter and advised me where I was going too far or not far enough. But the mistakes are all my own.

**Ann Benton** , February 2014

## Introduction

# Another book on parenting?

## Some things are much harder than they used to be

On a Friday morning during the wettest January on record, I stood outside the gates of our local primary school, where for over twenty-five years I have been visiting weekly to take the whole school for a time of singing and to rehearse the choir. Torrential rain was soaking my hair and my coat. Water was running down my neck as I fumbled amongst all the music in my bag for a post-it note on which is written the four-digit security code which will open the electronic

gate. I realise I should have known it by heart but on this occasion
memory failed me: they keep changing the code on account of
the ingenuity of eight-year olds. As my sodden fingers punched in
the code I reflected on the indisputable fact that some things are
much harder than they used to be.

Before a certain Wednesday in March 1996, people who
volunteered to help in schools had no such difficulties in gaining
entry. But Thomas Hamilton changed that when on March 13th
1996 he entered a primary school in Dunblane, Scotland and shot
sixteen children and a teacher. This is his legacy. Maybe security
codes on school gates have saved children's lives. I rather doubt it.
What I do know is that they have made people's lives harder.

Some things don't change.

I know the Dunblane massacre happened on a Wednesday
in March because, as with the assassination of JFK and other
shocking atrocities of my lifetime, I recall exactly where I was
when I heard about it. Somewhat poignantly, I was at an event
which annually celebrates primary school children in the town
where I live. The Schools' Music Festival assembles from all the
primary schools in the area a representation of young musical
talent. As trainer of the school choir I turn up every year with
my 16 best singers who have been drilled in a selection of songs
and who join a massed children's choir under a guest conductor's
baton and sing their little heads off before a paying audience.

An additional item on the programme on this occasion is
the combined orchestra. Keep in mind that these are ordinary
children aged eleven and less. Some of them have only been

learning their instruments for a matter of months. The look of frowning concentration on each of their faces as they scrape, pluck, bang or blow is magnificent. The sound is something else. Their rendition, one year, of Handel's Hallelujah Chorus caused me to stuff my handkerchief in my mouth in an effort to stifle a barely containable hoot of laughter. Here was a noise to make any listener question civilisation. And yet, as I glanced sidelong along my row, no one else was laughing. People were leaning forward with eager-eyed encouraging nods and smiles. Fingers twitched as occasionally a snatch of familiar rhythm or melody was identified. To be honest, there wasn't much to go on. At the last extraordinary chord, the auditorium erupted in thunderous applause and this was not, so I believe, with relief that the assault on the ear was over. This was genuine, unfettered delight and appreciation. I admired it most sincerely. I am all for encouraging effort. But the response was singularly that of an audience comprised almost totally of parents. Parental love is a wonderful thing. Generally it doesn't change. But it can also make a person blind, or in this case, deaf.

## Why am I writing another book on parenting?

For the two reasons exemplified in the above two stories.

Firstly, the world has changed. Just like getting into a primary school, parenting is harder than it used to be. The reasons behind some of the changes are generally well-intentioned with the safety and protection of children in mind. But, as I hope this book will demonstrate and as many parents acknowledge, the changes have made raising children harder work.

Secondly, the extraordinary and endearing love of parents for their children can make them blind to certain truths. They see their children; they love their children. But they don't always see what is going on.

Dr Aric Sigman in his book '*The Spoilt Generation*' spells out the problem and backs his thesis up with a considerable body of research. He talks about a 'landscape of spoiling' due to a retreat of parents from authority, sometimes under a banner of 'putting children first' or 'listening to children'. Because of this, boundaries have been removed and children are being robbed of a basic support system. His book is a plea to restore authority and counteract the growing sense of entitlement of the rising generation, which is not making them happier. It is not making their parents happier either.

I am not intending to write off a generation or to suggest that every child in Britain is a brat. But I hope to address the issues relating to a 'spoilt generation' in this book. I am writing particularly for Christians, although I know that some of the topics will be of concern to non-Christians as well. I regularly speak to a range of parents who are all too aware of the problem. I truly believe that God's ways are best for all people whatever their background and culture. Dr Sigman, not a believer, proves this by unwittingly making the case for a kind of parenting which has much in common with a Biblical worldview. Truth is truth wherever you find it and by God's common grace, unbelievers frequently make wise observations and suggestions.

Christian believers need to recognise, however, that the majority of modern parenting advice, however nice and cosy it sounds, is rooted in a worldview that is quite foreign to the

Bible and this very much affects the kind of advice that is given. The Bible is clear, for example, about parental authority and accountability, about the innate selfishness of every human heart and about absolute right and wrong. There are many in positions of influence who would hold quite other views. Sadly, I have discovered that some Christians have unconsciously swallowed the sugar-coated secularist pill and are blind to some serious flaws in much of what is written and promoted by health professionals, teachers and media parenting gurus. Other Christian parents, who are valiantly trying to follow the Bible's unfashionable precepts, are obliged to brace themselves because they are going very much against the tide. And sometimes it is hard.

Christians, whatever the prevailing political or cultural wind, are called to march to God's beat. As strangers and pilgrims here, and as we hope and pray that our children will join us in heaven, we have a serious purpose, and sooner or later that will mean in various ways going against the tide.

So here is another book on parenting. What I have tried to do is look at a plethora of issues on which thinking, Bible-believing parents may find themselves at odds with their non-Christian neighbours. Some, but not all, of these issues are controversial. Where there is divided opinion I have not backed off but have attempted to bring Biblical principles to bear. Let the reader decide.

In writing this book I also want to state at the outset that I am aware that there are plenty of non-Christians who do a pretty good job of bringing up decent, well-behaved children. Of course there are. Such parents have recognised and applied good sense and ignored nonsense and that policy has paid off. But there is a huge difference between believers and unbelievers in motivation, ambition and destination. So there will be distinctions which we need to acknowledge. And there will be concerns which are of no interest to those who have no concept of eternity. Christians know there is more at stake here than worldly prosperity and a healthy lifestyle.

If, in the course of the argument, I seem to be occasionally harsh or sweeping, I beg the reader's pardon. I write out of the very warmest of hearts towards today's parents and even more, towards their children. And I do so because I stand on God's infallible word and delight to see Jesus Christ glorified in Christian family life. My aim is to warn the unwary and encourage the stout-hearted.

So let us begin.

# Chapter 1

# Mother knows best (and Father too)

## A discussion of parenthood and parental authority

*Fiona got a surprise when she opened Jack's lunchbox: the packet of crisps was lying there untouched. Crisps were a rare treat and Fiona had included them in the lunch as a special birthday surprise so Fiona was very puzzled. There was a folded letter under the crisps; it was from Jack's teacher. It read thus:*

*'Dear parents and carers,*

*At Larch Avenue School we are very interested in the health of our children. In the light of a recent Ofsted inspection, we are aiming to improve the eating habits of our pupils. Some of the items in your child's lunchbox were deemed unsuitable and were therefore temporarily removed by our midday supervisors. They are being returned to you with the request that in future you include in the lunchbox only items from our "healthy eating list", which we are enclosing…'*

## Who needs parents?

Apparently there are people who have your child's interest at heart more than you, the parent, do. From the contents of the lunchbox to advice on sex and sexuality there are plenty of professionals ready to override the authority of a parent.

What do parents know anyway? The long-running campaign by successive governments to get more mothers back into (taxable) paid employment assumed that more affordable childcare was the answer to every parent's prayer. No one asked the question: what is better for the child? It was taken for granted that a childcare professional could do as good or a better job of raising a child than a parent. When it was reported in February 2014 that 'the gender gap is closing' (i.e. between men and women in full-time paid employment) this was assumed to be a very good thing.

The question of women taking on salaried employment outside the home is not the issue here. I am not making the case for mothers to stay permanently tied to the kitchen sink and nursery. I am perfectly well aware of the reasons why women return to the workplace, the most pressing of which may well be a financial one. The issue here is the message about motherhood.

Motherhood has rarely been so undervalued. And it is no coincidence that simultaneously the authority of parents has never been so undermined. If schools can raid and confiscate items from lunchboxes, how long before they consider it in your child's interest to vet or ban your child's reading material as politically incorrect or bigoted?

The Children Act of 2004 does rather patronisingly acknowledge 'the importance of parents in improving the well-being of children' but the tone of the act is to magnify the role of other agencies as the ones who really know what is best for children. While government, media and the woman at the checkout in Sainsbury's are ready to blame parents for everything from obesity to looting, there has been a systematic and sustained attack on the essential and benign authority of mothers and fathers. It has been a two pronged campaign, proclaiming simultaneously that

a. Anyone can care for a child.

b. Parents do not necessarily know what is best for their children; others know better and should always be able to override what a mere parent thinks.

Is it any wonder that many twenty-first century parents are paranoid, guilty and anxious?

## Biblical motherhood

The Bible takes a different view on parents. When the infant Moses is discovered floating in a basket on the Nile by a princess of Egypt, his sister Miriam is on hand to suggest the best possible childcare—Moses' own mother.

So without any intended slight on fathers, whose crucial importance we shall recognise later in this chapter, let us examine the Biblical stance on motherhood, so easily devalued in our times. If you want to get back to basics in the Bible there is no better place than the book of Genesis, which has plenty of mothering issues.

## The significance of motherhood

It sticks out a mile in a read-through of Genesis that most of what we hear about women concerns the bearing and raising of children. It is worth pointing out that this aspect of Genesis is massively different from other ancient Mesopotamian writings, in whose birth reports there is a significant absence of the mention of mothers. Quite counter-culturally even in those days, the Bible is saying that mothers have a big part to play. While the pre-eminent human relationship is marriage, which is permanent (Genesis 2:24) and children will grow and leave the parental home to form their own marriages, yet for a married woman the bearing and raising of children is extremely significant, probably the most significant thing she will do in her life.

So when motherhood is tellingly referred to as a 'career break', spot the lie. It would be closer to the truth to say that a mother's paid employment is a 'motherhood break'.

The near obsession with procreation from Genesis 12 on is because of the promise to Abraham. When God does something about this sad, fallen world, he does it through a family.

And so begins the unfolding of the redemption plan which would culminate in the arrival of the Saviour. And in Genesis there is a good deal of ink used in telling how this whole thing will get going. To have lots of descendants you have to start with one. This one is a long time coming and there are various false starts. Abraham thinks it will be maybe through his nephew Lot, or his faithful servant Eliezer, or through the Egyptian maid Hagar. Thrice wrong!

The problem is the barrenness of Sarah and yet God has Sarah in mind as the mother. He is quite clear that the promised child will be born, within wedlock, to Sarah (Genesis 18:10). Sarah is crucial to this plan. Mothers are as important as fathers. Any old woman will not do.

In the next generation there is huge attention given to finding the right wife for Isaac because the mother of the next generation is also crucial to the redemption plan. When Isaac and Rebekah are married, Rebekah's barrenness becomes the focus of Isaac's prayers. Why? Because of the promise made to Abraham—the plan for the redemption of the world.

The line continued, as we know, to David and to David's greater Son, but the mothers in that line right up to Mary had a crucial and significant part to play.

Obviously none of us can attribute the same significance to our mothering as Mary could as the mother of Jesus. Yet the Bible is clear (and this book will go on to explain) that the God who wants godly offspring from his people's marriages (Malachi 2:15) has assigned crucial functions to mothers which go beyond the delivery room.

## God's delightful gift

From the examples already mentioned it is evident that the Bible views fertility as God's gift. Sarah is barren but at God's say-so she bears a child. Rebekah is barren but when Isaac prays, God answers his prayer and Rebekah becomes pregnant (Genesis 25:21). Rachel is barren and complains to her husband Jacob that her sister Leah is having babies but she is not. And Jacob says, 'Am I in the place of God, who has withheld from you the fruit of the womb?'

It is important to make this point in an age when we think we have taken our fertility into our own hands. I do not want to argue against contraception, because it is clear from the Bible that God allows us the use of means in order to live wisely. However, we need to take care that our use of birth control is not merely for material and selfish reasons, following the pattern of the world where babies are treated as commodities to be brought in to suit our convenience and lifestyle. One of the key purposes of marriage is to bring children into the world. Motherhood is God's gift and it is one of his greatest. When a child arrives into a family, as it were, 'unplanned', believing parents will (if not immediately) rejoice in the fact that God is the great family planner. To spend years in the raising of children is a fine and godly thing to do. And as you raise children to be decent, kind, useful citizens you are doing the world a favour as well.

It is also important to recognise that our children are God's gift to us, because there may be times when you survey your offspring and sigh deeply or wonder if one of them was switched in the hospital! There may be times of remorse and regrets. Perhaps you never thought when you rocked the cradle that it would come to this. Then is the time to remember that motherhood is God's gift. He chose you to bear this child and raise it. It may be a tough assignment at times but it is still a precious gift.

But motherhood is also delightful. When Sarah finally gave birth at the age of ninety, she called the child Isaac, which means laughter. She may have been recalling the time the previous year when the Lord had visited them and spoken of the coming happy event and she had laughed in cynical disbelief. But now when this first-time mother, who thought this could never happen to her, cradles a baby in her arms, she says, 'God has made laughter for me.' It is supremely delightful to hold your own little baby, to have him wrap his fingers around your finger.

This is one of the many good gifts that God in his common grace gives to people, just because he is generous. Unlike the world, which can give the impression that motherhood is a chore or a bore, Christian mothers can revel and continue revelling in the extraordinary gift of God. Thank him and enjoy his good gift. With all the pain and problems, with all the onerous and serious responsibility, we should never forget to enjoy our children. When difficulties arise and we are tempted to say (with very bad theology) 'what did I do to deserve this?' we should also look at our children and wonder like Sarah that, sinners as we are, God has brought us laughter. Grace teaches us to observe, 'What did I do to deserve this?'

## The nature of nurture

One further point about motherhood from the book of Genesis:
It is nurturant. After all the build-up to the birth of the promised
son to Abraham and Sarah, it is an event which is given pretty
short shrift in the account (Genesis 21:2). The event given
attention is the party to celebrate the fact that Isaac was weaned,
which was probably a few years later, since it was the custom for
women to breastfeed their children for years rather than months.
Many children did not survive infancy so it was fitting to celebrate
the fact that a child had come through its most vulnerable stage
and was ready to be launched into a wider arena.

Sarah's comment in Genesis 21:7 is significant here. 'Who
would have said to Abraham that Sarah would nurse children?' It
is not merely the giving birth but the successful suckling (nursing)
of a child that is wonderful. Sarah has not only borne a child but
nursed him.

The message is this: motherhood is not merely the bearing of
children but the nurturing of them. Adoptive mothers need to
take this on board. The nurturing is the really significant thing.

When the apostle Paul compares his care for the church to
the care of a mother in 1 Thessalonians 2:6–9, he gives some
insight into the nature of motherly nurture. He talks about gentle,
joyful, selfless care. Nurturant means more than physical care
at a mother's breast. Psychologists acknowledge that the value
of breastfeeding is not just about all the goodies that the milk
contains to promote growth, but the sense of security and the
bonding that is established through prolonged and regular times
of being held close. This is vital to an infant. And those who are

obliged to use a bottle can still do that. The word 'caring' which Paul uses to describe the work of a mother literally means 'keep warm'. It summarizes all that cherishing, feeding, home-making work that a mother brings to her family. What a mother gives to her infant cannot easily be replaced by what a professional child-carer, however well-qualified, does. The work of a mother is to care. Just as she provided a home and sustenance in her womb, so that same caring goes on into life until the child can take care of himself.

## The crucial importance of fathers

What about fathers? Where do they fit in? The so-called equality agenda has aimed to render all gender distinctions arbitrary and gender roles sexist. At one level the importance of fatherhood has been acknowledged through comparatively recent employment legislation making paternity leave a recognised obligation. Many young fathers have appreciated this opportunity to spend extended time with their newborn child and in assimilating the adjustment that an addition to the family entails. So we have the new Dad, who cuts the umbilical cord, changes nappies, gets up in the night, pushes the pram and shares the childcare.

I don't deride it. There is no reason why a father should not do any of the above. And Biblical fatherhood was never designed to be distant. Note Paul's word to fathers in the Colossian church: 'Do not embitter your children, or they will become discouraged.' One certain way to embitter a child is to refuse to get involved.

But there is a problem. Mothers and fathers in the secular worldview have become virtually interchangeable. Meanwhile marriage as a lifelong heterosexual union has been subject to unreasonable attack, despite all the evidence that children thrive best when raised by a married mother and father.

Who cares who raises a child? Two men? Two women? One woman? One man? Not only has distinctive, nurturing motherhood been undermined by the equality agenda but fatherhood has, paradoxically, been turned into motherhood as men are encouraged to find their feminine side.

One of the reasons that Paul addresses his instructions on family life (Ephesians 6:4; Colossians 3:21) to fathers and not to mothers is that the Biblical model for the family is that the father is the head of the family. He is the one who will give an account to God, the ultimate Father, about his leadership of the family. As head of the family after God's pattern he is the principal provider and protector. In Genesis 2 man was created from the dust of the earth, to work; woman was created from the man to be his helper. One of the ways that manly provision and protection might be expressed in the present day is that he earns the money so that the mother of his children can, as much as possible while the children are young, remain at home doing her caring work. Different roles but one is not more important than the other.

Of course, there are situations and reasons where this pattern may be modified—there is some elasticity in the Biblical model. But since God's design for family life was that a child should have a mother and a father and since there are inbuilt, indisputable differences between the genders, it seems reasonable to suggest that God wanted all the best aspects of masculinity and femininity respectively brought into the parenting mix.

Generally, (and I stress that word) mothers and fathers intuitively play, communicate and discipline in different ways. Fathers tend to be more practical, logical and focused on performance, end-products and consequences; mothers tend to be more sympathetic and relational. These approaches are complementary and bring a healthy balance to family life. United around a common policy, a masculine father and a feminine mother make an effective team. While the Bible reminds fathers not to be harsh, it promotes fatherly involvement. If any reader doubts the crucial importance of fathers to the raising of well-adjusted, well-behaved children, talk to any schoolteacher.

Raising children is a team effort. This may call for a good deal of selflessness on the part of a father who perseveres in a job he does not much like in order to be a faithful, providing father. It also may call for selflessness on the part of a mother who for a number of years is largely home-based and feels deprived of the camaraderie of the office or the worldly recognition of a salary and promotion. But a little bit of selflessness doesn't do us any harm. God's pattern for the family is one which recognises that God has made man and woman different. His pattern is one which works. If it upsets feminists of your acquaintance, that really is not your problem.

### Who cares most?

The Bible's creation account tells us the correct nurturing environment for a child. Did you ever wonder why God did not create Adam and Eve as children and put them in the garden to run about like innocents or like Romulus and Remus to be suckled by a she-wolf and fed by a woodpecker? If various enlightenment thinkers are correct, would they not have thrived in their innocency, 'trailing clouds of glory'? But God first created the man and the woman and then gave them children. Eve's words were, 'I have gotten a man with the help of the Lord' (Genesis 4:1). Children were not dropped into the world but created and brought forth in the most intimate way imaginable to be protected and cared for by their parents. Here Adam and Eve were fulfilling part of the creation mandate to be fruitful and increase in number (Genesis 1:28). Themselves created in God's image, they were to reproduce more image-bearers, so that the world would be peopled by those who reflected God. This is the job of the parent.

In a fallen world the new creation mandate of Matthew 28:19–20 mirrors that of Genesis. We are to grow children for God. They have been born into this world and we want more than anything that they be born again into the kingdom of God to reflect his image as new creation.

Children need parents. If they needed parents at creation they certainly need them now. They need them because they are weak and need protection; they are ignorant and need instruction; they are wayward and need correction; they are lost and need direction. That is the job of a mother and a father, working together to supply that protection, instruction, correction and direction. They make a good team because they have complementary gifts and they both really care about what they are doing. I am not arguing that a parent can never trust anyone else with childcare. There is scope for appropriate delegation as a child grows. But it is important to recognise who are the ultimate carers: it is the parents. Their children are special to them in a way they could not be to anyone else. They care most.

## A word to single parents

Not all the readers of this book will be married. I admire the selflessness of those who are doing their utmost to raise their children decently and doing it by themselves. But the many single parents I meet would be the first to admit that raising a child on your own is difficult and exhausting. They know it would be easier with two. They know their situation is not ideal. A strong and supportive wider family (especially grandparents), a good network of friends, plus a loving local church community will go some way to plugging the gaps. And Christian experience bears out the wonderful Bible truth that God meets us in our failures and helplessness and works even these for our good. He hears our prayers, forgives our sins and renews our strength as we wait on him. But he does not turn the clock back.

Children thrive with married parents. That is God's plan and all the research backs it up. That does not mean that children of single parents cannot thrive. It means it is harder work; but it is not game over. God is kind. Ultimately he is in charge, not statistics. Lean on him, walk with him, learn from him.

## Parents are experts

In these days when we are awash with professional experts, it is also good for all parents to keep in mind that they are the true experts on their own children. Sometimes when I give talks on parenting, I am confronted during the question time by a troubled parent with a very particular current problem. In the context of a general public question time the best that somebody like me can hope for is to reiterate principles and give some broad brush stroke applications based on experience and observation. But as I often say, I have not met their child and even if I spent a day in their house I would not know their child like they know the child. They are the experts. I hear myself give some general suggestion and I see the disappointment in their eyes—'Does she think we haven't tried that already?' What do I know after all? They are the experts on their own child. That doesn't mean that they know all the answers: experts are still learners. But they can be sure of this: they know their child better than anyone else. Since the child's first cry, they have been watching and interpreting. A toilet-training mother knows when her toddler wants the potty before the child himself does. That is why as experts they are in a very good position to assess and make decisions about their children's needs and how they should be met.

The Christian parent has the best possible model in God himself, the Eternal Father. (More of this in chapter 4). The parent imagery is a recurrent theme in Scripture. One good example is in Hosea 11 when God talks of himself as the father of the nation of Israel. The picture is of a devoted father recalling teaching his child to walk, holding his hand, comforting and healing when he hurt himself, feeding and protecting him. This is a relationship of tenderness, built on knowledge and an enduring commitment, whatever happens. Only parents can bring that level of care.

## The authority of parents

Not only are the parents the ultimate carers of their children under God, but they are also under God the ultimate authority. Authority is generally considered a bit of a dirty word these days. But the Bible pattern is quite clear that parents have authority over their children. The family is structured so that the young can be protected, instructed, corrected and directed. And those things cannot be done without authority. This is not a harsh and cruel authority; it is possible to use authority without being a bully. On the contrary, Biblical parental authority is benign and, aligned with tender knowledge and care, creates the best possible context for healthy development. It is evidenced at its best in a child who respects and listens to his parents, who takes correction and is obedient. Far from being oppressive, it is joyous and life-giving.

> 'Listen to your father who gave you life,
> and do not despise your mother when she is old.
> Buy truth, and do not sell it;
> buy wisdom, instruction, and understanding.
> The father of the righteous will greatly rejoice;
> he who fathers a wise son will be glad in him.
> Let your father and mother be glad;
> let her who bore you rejoice.'
>
> Proverbs 23:22–25

That is the standard of Biblical family life where father and mother work together to raise wise and disciplined children who love the truth.

## Some practical inferences and applications

1. It is quite possible in our busy lives to make mothering and fathering a matter of maintenance and administration. Has this happened to you? What aspects of mothering or fathering mentioned in this chapter have you been forgetting?

2. Consider how present trends which disrespect or devalue parents have affected your thinking. What are the things that you the parent can do best for your child? Are you doing them?

3. Know that you are the expert on your child. Spend a little time reflecting on his/her character, development and present needs. Turn these into prayer.

## For further reading

- 'The Essence of Family' by Kirsten Birkett (Matthias Media)

- 'Recovering Biblical Manhood and Womanhood' edited by John Piper and Wayne Grudem. (Crossway Books)

- 'Who needs Parents?' by Patricia Morgan, (Institute of Economic Affairs)

- 'The Spoilt Generation' by Dr Aric Sigman (Piatkus)

# Chapter 2

# The myth of self-esteem

## How an urban myth turned parenting upside down and made us afraid of our children

*Once upon a time there was a little girl, a very ordinary little girl. She did not win at games or get 'A-stars' and she was sad to be so very ordinary. One day as she was shaking out her breakfast cereal a free gift fell from inside the packet onto her plate. It looked like a pink plastic figurine but when she pulled open the cellophane a real live fairy stood on the table. The fairy said, 'Annabelle, you are not ordinary ; you are special. And so that you will know how special you are I am giving you this magic mirror. You will be able to be anything and do anything if you just have this mirror.' The magic mirror worked like this—it showed the person who looked in it herself as she would like to be—beautiful, clever, accomplished and popular so when she looked at herself she was frankly impressed. It ran by batteries and the batteries were charged by getting other people to rub it. So as Annabelle went about that day, her priority was to get people to rub her mirror, so that when she went home at night and when she got up in the morning she looked at herself and saw this fantastic person and felt very, very happy. She was actually still just an ordinary person. She was no better at games and did not get higher grades in tests (the fairy lied) but she was OK with that now because her mirror told its own story and the mirror was the most important indicator in her life. If she neglected her mirror so it got dirty; if she forgot to ask people to rub it, it showed her as drab and boring so the mirror and its state became a major pre-occupation and once she found that many of her friends had mirrors, it was an unspoken agreement between them all that they would always rub each other's mirrors. Anyone who would not join in this activity would be completely ostracised. In the end Annabelle only chose to go to places and mix with people who would polish her mirror and keep its batteries charged.*

That story is a parable about the way in which in the last three decades we have been systematically taught to raise our children and relate to each other. Our children are to be continually affirmed and made to feel good about themselves. This activity is otherwise known as building self-esteem. Building self-esteem is looked upon as a crucial goal for parents, teachers, employers and any other kind of 'investors in people'.

One example of this is to be found in current practice at children's parties. I was allowed to help at one recently and was delighted to discover that the old favourite 'Pass the parcel' is still being played. I loved this game myself as a child. It has a very simple concept. A small gift is wrapped in several layers of paper. The parcel is passed around a circle of children while music is played. The music stops randomly and whoever is holding the parcel at that point takes off a layer of wrapping, in the hope that it will be the final layer. If it is not, the music resumes and the parcel is passed around again.

But contemporary parents will note two ways in which the old game has been adapted for the twenty-first century child. Firstly, there is some kind of prize with every layer. All must have prizes. No one must be upset. Secondly, and more alarmingly: the stopping of the music is not random! No, the operator of the sound system deliberately cheats to ensure that every child gets a turn at removing a layer of paper, and thereby getting a prize. Even smart participating children (I observed) catch on to the system and are aware that once they have had their 'turn' at unwrapping, they won't get another. It tends to rather reduce the fun, don't you think? But it won't damage self-esteem.

A low level of self esteem is said to be associated with emotional damage that is in turn said to cause a range of social problems from crime to teenage pregnancy. Most of us have heard this concept bandied about in the media, in school, or at work. Yet until comparatively recently not only was lack of self-esteem not perceived as a problem, the term itself had nothing to do with emotional health.

A computer search of citations of the word 'self-esteem' in British newspapers did not find it used once in 1980. In 1986 it was only used three times. By 1990 the figure rose to 103. By 2000 there were a staggering 3,328 references to self-esteem. Now it is a common-place word and a common-place concept. And always it is linked to emotional health and well-being. It has achieved the status of an urban myth. In this chapter I want to try and examine some of the things we have been taught to believe which contribute to this myth and affect our parenting.

## Here are three lies:

### Lie Number 1: You have to love yourself before you can love others

I put this one first because it is one I have heard most frequently, even from the lips of Christians. They wrap it up in the Christian language of 'love your neighbour as yourself' and suggest that. that commandment infers that you 'have to love yourself first'. But actually this is straight from the definitely-not-Christian textbooks of Carl Rogers. It can be summed up in the cliché: I'm OK, you're OK.' As long as a person thinks he is OK, he will be inclined to think others are OK and be OK and open and warm with them. That is the theory in a nutshell.

The problem with that statement is that it has behind it an assumption that we need to be taught, helped or encouraged to love ourselves. But my first observation is that we all love ourselves pretty well quite naturally. Little babies love themselves enough to cry when they are hungry; we all love ourselves enough to make sure that we take food and clothe ourselves and keep comfortable. We spend our lives doing that. Surely the Biblical command is simply to point out that God requires us to care as much for the needs of others as we already do, quite naturally, for ourselves.

My second observation is that people who love themselves a lot are the least likely to care about others. You only have to watch an episode of the popular BBC programme 'The Apprentice' to discover how very unattractive and unloving an inflated self-love and self-promotion can be.

My third observation is that many, many of the people who have done most for human-kind have put themselves through a considerable amount of sweat and toil and did not think about themselves at all. What they thought of themselves was the last thing on their minds.

## Lie number 2: Affirmation of the self is the central essential element of the good life

Behind this lie is the assumption that there is no authority higher than the self. Neither is there anyone to please higher than the self. The central principle behind the self-esteem movement is the over-arching moral significance of the self: 'me'. 'If it feels right'. This is me-ism, caricatured in the old Carly Simon song: 'You're so vain, you probably think this song is about you.' Actually the last few generations have been trained to think that everything is about 'me'. Whereas ideologies of the past, especially Christianity, have demanded denial of the self for the sake of a higher interest, there is now a drive only to self-refer. Everything is assessed as to how it affects 'me'. There is no opinion of me more valid than my own. No one has the right to comment on my behaviour.

Again, a former worldview would have contained a concept of accountability to someone much higher than the self. From this outside perspective came a highly developed sense of right and wrong which existed absolutely whether or not anyone either liked it or conformed to it.

But in the increasing atheistic secularism of the last half-century, our culture has cut the strings of this outside higher authority and standard. If there is no God to please we will please ourselves. Now if there is no God to please there is also no God to be pleased, so I have to do that for myself. I have to be pleased with myself. I have to affirm myself or else by a tacit agreement with others make sure that I live and breathe affirmation to others while they do the same for me. This is like the people in my parable who polish each other's mirrors. And the more of this affirmation the better. Once people had to do something amazing and then maybe someone might applaud, now we want, even need, the applause without doing anything at all.

Note the contrast with Jesus. When Jesus talked about prayer and giving he commended the act of secret praying and secret giving. Plenty in those days did it for the affirmation of men. They get their reward, says Jesus. But the real thing is what goes on in secret, away from human eyes. And the God who sees what is done in secret is the audience that counts.

But when we believe this lie that the only place for affirmation is ourselves, we are a culture doomed to a continuous quest for affirmation. We have discounted anything above ourselves.

Do you see where this gets us? We have to affirm and never

discriminate. We must all polish each other's mirrors. And as parents we must continually polish our children's mirrors. The problem is that sometimes we just have the passing thought that some attitude or behaviour is not so great, or is even bad. But we become nervous about saying it. Because to make a moral judgment or a value judgment i.e. to say 'that is wrong' would not be very affirming. It might upset someone. So we tend to keep quiet or if we correct we wrap our correction up in such an affirming bracket that the correction itself is diluted. In effect many parents are afraid of their children; or at least they fear their children's displeasure. That is why they continually ask their children if they 'would like to do' something, rather than give them a straight instruction. There was a time when children thought they had to please their parents. Now parents think it is their job to please their children.

This has happened because we have made the self the highest reference point in our lives. We have believed the lie that the central goal of life is to be happy and to feel good about ourselves (and those two things go together). So in education all must have prizes. Parenting courses teach parents not to condemn certain behaviour as wrong—merely as a 'sad choice'. And we have children who are flattered, pampered, who can't take correction, whose fragile egos are hyper-sensitive, who cannot deal with the indifference of others, who expect to be entertained, who have a massive sense of entitlement and a very small sense of service. It is not in one sense their fault. They have been trained that way, nurtured by a generation of people who thought that the one thing you must not do is damage a child's self-esteem.

## Lie number 3: Thinking badly of yourself is bad for you

The self-esteem myth leads you to pursue self-affirmation at all costs. There is a common tendency to link a whole range of social evils with low self-esteem. But this is taken for granted rather than proven by scientific research. There is an extraordinary absence of any data to prove an association of low self-esteem with social problems. But for the self-esteem movement research and science have little importance. If they feel it to be so, it is so.

The result is that we have all sorts of ridiculous idea like teachers not marking work wrong, when it actually is. It is very discouraging, so the ideology goes, for a child to see his exercise book returned to him with crosses on it. So there are some schools where teachers tick what is correct and leave blank what is incorrect.

In a home setting there are parents who systematically cheat to let their children win at games. This is done because they do not want a child to be sad or feel a failure. Parents do not confront bad behaviour for the same reason. They excuse, they deny, they distract.

They think that failure and guilt is bad for you. And so they avoid situations where they or their children might feel guilty. In so doing they abandon one of the great mechanisms for learning—getting it wrong. Well, of course false guilt is unhelpful, but genuine guilt is very, very good for you. It is there to cause you to reflect on your behaviour and to adjust it.

There is a famous play by J B Priestley called 'An Inspector Calls'. It is set on the occasion of a family celebration—a very prosperous and self-important family. But the inspector, whom they assume to be from the police, arrives and announces the tragic death of a young woman, in whose demise each member of the family in different ways and over a period of time has had a hand. They are made to face up to their responsibility and their guilt. They are sobered and frightened as they face the truth about themselves as human beings. But once the genuineness and authority of the Inspector is questioned—he is not really a police inspector; no such girl died—they start to feel better. They can deny and go on as they were before. Or so some of them think. Only the daughter of the family acknowledges that the guilt is real whether or not there were criminal charges or public exposure. She wants to use what they have learned to change. Guilt can be good for you bringing with it the opportunity for forgiveness and a fresh start.

But if we cannot occasionally think badly of ourselves, if we always have to edit the tape so that we come out as right, if we are only hearing the affirmation of others and switching off the voice which questions our right to the moral high ground, then we end up with a distorted view of reality and a superficial facade of our own worth.

## But what about praise and encouragement?

Well, exactly. Do not read me as saying there is no place for praise and encouragement when raising a child. Explicit praise is an excellent training tool because it reinforces a desired behaviour while strengthening the warmth of a relationship. Children actually do like to please the significant adult in the room. And without encouragement a child's spirit is crushed (Proverbs 12:25). But it is precisely because these are such valuable tools in child-rearing that we must not devalue them, by using them randomly and meaninglessly. There is a difference between praise and flattery. Praise relates to actual worth; it is a due response to something worthy observed, whether in attitude, effort or achievement. Encouragement is what happens when someone is genuinely praised. Flattery has a more sinister motive. It is not linked to anything specific and is often a manipulative tool so that the flatterer can get what he or she wants. It bears no relation to truth or desert and therefore nothing is learned, though the object of flattery may feel temporarily very happy. But it is also dangerous:

> 'A lying tongue hates its victims,
> and a flattering mouth works ruin.'          Proverbs 26:28

> 'A man who flatters his neighbor
> spreads a net for his feet.'          Proverbs 29:5

So of course parents will recognise and verbally affirm good performance and behaviour and let their children know in many different ways how very special they are to them. It is also crucially important to acknowledge and praise effort. But, if they are wise, they will also respond quite coolly to anything they consider unworthy or inappropriate. Not everything your child produces is 'wonderful'. You only raise your child's thirst for affirmation and general sense of entitlement by saying so. On the other hand the Bible reminds us that a warranted rebuke for unacceptable behaviour, while harder to give, is a kinder response than wheedling flattery (Proverbs 28:23).

So, what is a healthy self-image and how is it achieved? Here are three points of Biblical truth:

## 1. Every human being wears the manufacturer's label

The Bible says that you don't hold a mirror, you *are* a mirror. When the Genesis account of the creation of the world gets to the bit about humankind we find that God said, 'Let us make man in our image.' Human beings were and are made image-bearers, reflecting the God who made them. They are therefore deserving of the utmost dignity and respect regardless of appearance, performance, creed or culture. This is why the first and greatest philanthropists this world has ever seen have been those who held to a Judaeo-Christian worldview. When, in the nineteenth century, Lord Shaftesbury worked tirelessly to stop the practice of children being sent up chimneys or down mines, he did so not from any sentimental view of children, but because he knew that every child is made in the image of God.

Parents tend to think that their own children are pretty special. But here is what makes your child really special: he or she is made in the image of God. She doesn't need to wear designer label clothes; she already wears a designer label, that of one made by the immortal, invisible Creator.

Now we all know that human beings don't behave like God and that is because they have as a race turned their back of God. You have daily evidence that this is true of your children too. This mirror is cracked and deeply flawed, but it still reflects. It increasingly reflects whatever we worship during our lives, either the living God, or whatever else we worship (Jeremiah 2:5; 2 Corinthians 3:18). When we worship and esteem ourselves we become narrow, superficial and increasingly self-centred. When we encourage our children to do so, we do them no favours.

## 2. Receiving unconditional love enables us to function in the world and love others

The Bible is one big story about the matchless love of God for rebellious human kind. When we were God's enemies, he sent his Son to take the punishment for our treasonable acts of rebellion. That is unconditional love; that is grace. As image bearers we know a little bit about this if we are parents. With relatively few tragic exceptions, parents are passionate about their children. They nurture them selflessly; they delight in their company; they forbear and forgive; they support them and frequently pay out for them. That is a small-scale reflection of God who is the ultimate Father.

Now it is a well-attested fact that a fundamental need of every baby is not just food and clothing but love. Maternal deprivation in the early years, as it used to be called, is something very hard to make up in later life. It is undeniably psychologically damaging. Only a mother or father, or someone taking on all that that means, can give what a developing baby needs most in order to thrive—unconditional love. While it is not true to say that you have to love yourself before you can love others, it is true to say that unless you have received love you will have little to give. The love of a parent is immeasurably valuable to a healthy self-image. That kind of investment in the earliest years of life is something no-one can take away from a growing human-being. But the best of parents let you down; they are not always there for you; they die; they disappear; they are helpless in many situations.

Human fatherly and motherly love is just a picture of the love of God. His love is described as unfailing and it is proved in the death of Jesus Christ on the cross so that helpless hopeless mortals could be restored to a relationship with Almighty God. There is a whole lot of stuff that goes on in that restored relationship which I don't have time to dwell on here. Suffice it to say that the knowledge that God loves me, not for being good (even if I were) but despite my failings, releases me to be honest, glad and generous to others.

Our children, if signally loved by us the parents, will be well-placed to make warm and healthy relationships with others. That is a huge part of a parent's work from day one of a child's life. But our children also need to be instructed from their earliest days in the matchless, unfailing love of their heavenly Father.

## 3. It is the meta-narrative which gives a wholesome sense of direction and purpose

What I mean by meta-narrative is that there is a big story going on. In contrast to the self-esteem myth which makes it all about you, the Bible has an over-arching story which is gloriously not about you or about me. That does not make you and me irrelevant or insignificant—on the contrary we have a part to play in this story. We will either be those who bow the knee to Jesus Christ now and live our lives to honour him and enjoy knowing him and making him known, or we will be those who live our lives in wilful ignorance of him and in a fantasy of our own making in which we rule our own worlds, but who on the last dreadful day will be obliged all the same to acknowledge that Jesus Christ is Lord. That is true for our children too, of course.

This is the significance of teaching our children Bible truth, more of which will be said in a later chapter. They need the meta-narrative. It comes initially in the form of Bible stories but these should at an early stage be linked into the one big story of redemption. This is the route to raising children who happily accept themselves as God made them and embrace their place in the universe. The first couple of questions in the children's catechism put us all on the road to a sane and meaningful life:

Q: Who made you?

A: God made me.

Q: What else did God make?

A: God made all things.

Q: Why did God make you and all things?

A: For his own glory.

We are surrounded in this world by those who deny that meta-narrative. In doing so, they condemn themselves to a life without purpose or direction apart from that of surviving and trying against the odds to be happy. Such a life is characterised by moral blindness of which they are barely even aware.

## The faith alternative

If you live by faith in the Son of God who loved you and gave himself for you, you know where you are going. Self-esteem is a non-issue because you are more interested in what God thinks of you than in what other people think.

Instead of self-esteem you have:

- Self-distrust—because you know your capacity for getting things wrong and this prevents you from ever, ever being smug, because if God has opened your eyes and poured his love on you it certainly was not what you deserved.

- Self-examination—not in some maudlin way but always rigorously in keeping with the truth of Scripture. You have an outside absolute not only to encourage you but also to challenge you. That is one reason why believers in the Lord Jesus Christ so frequently love to be listening to God's word explained. It sets them right again and crucially, they did not make it up to make themselves feel better. The Bible is itself described as a mirror and the right use of that mirror is when it exposes something wrong to admit and to change (James 1:22–25). This is not a magic mirror but a real one which holds out real hope. Because where sin is admitted and confessed and repented of, there is real forgiveness from the proper authority.

- Self-denial—Jesus named this as the very foundation of discipleship (Matthew 16:24). Along with that challenging invitation he gave the most inspiring promise that 'whoever loses his life for my sake will find it.' God is no man's debtor.

- Self-forgetfulness—since as a person renewed by God's Holy Spirit, you find your life driven by the two great commands—to love God and to love your neighbour. The first one puts everything in its right place. Rather than esteeming yourself or even thinking in those terms, you are esteeming God and you are esteeming other people. You won't find as many books on those subjects as you will on building self-esteem, but there is no happier way to live.

We know that faith is the gift of God. It is not in our gift. Our job as parents is to model the life of faith (by our own self-distrust, self-examination, self-denial and self-forgetfulness) and instruct our children in the truth. Beyond that we pray that God will open their eyes to see the Saviour and follow him.

## Some practical inferences and applications

1. Do your children crave affirmation? Perhaps you have been over-affirming. Develop a place in your family life for some healthy neglect, i.e. regular times when your children amuse themselves out of sight and earshot in bedroom or garden. What begins as a discipline may become a source of joy for them and sanity for you. They can learn a lot by being left to themselves for a bit, not least how to function without a continual affirmative running commentary from you.

2. Do you allow your children to fail? Do they always win when you play games? They need to learn to lose at games without sulking, as well as how to win at games without being insufferable. Practice makes perfect. What about other types of failure? Do you allow your children to get things wrong? Model to them what to do with guilt. Explain to them that we are all sinners and therefore fail on a daily basis. Teach them that the answer to guilt is forgiveness and that, to quote the

excellent Richard Sibbes 'There is more grace in Christ than there is sin in us.'

## For further reading

'The Big Ego-trip' by Glynn Harrison (IVP)

'Therapy Culture' by Frank Furedi (Routledge)

'The Narcissism Epidemic' by Jean M. Twenge (Free Press)

# Chapter 3

# Right and Wrong— who says so?

## The muddle created by relativism

*A travelling salesman in the US was working away from home, on the road in the State of Illinois. His wife meanwhile was watching the television and caught a news report which said that chaos was being caused on the interstate in Illinois by some crazy motorist driving on the wrong side of the road, down the interstate. Immediately the woman telephoned her husband on his mobile, knowing that he was likely to be in that area.*

*'Do be careful, dear,' she said, 'The news says there's a madman on the interstate driving on the wrong side of the road.'*

*'One madman?' said her husband. 'There are hundreds of them!'*

That story illustrates the issue precisely. Is right and wrong a personal category or an objective one? In the case of the right and wrong side of the road, of course the answer to that question is different according to where in the world the question is asked. But what about right and wrong behaviour? Are there some actions and attitudes which are absolutely right and others which are absolutely wrong? Or do we have to define those words for ourselves, as a matter of taste and preference?

This is a deeply serious philosophical question. It is also a practical question if you are a parent. Whether you have a toddler or a teenager you will come up against this question. In their different ways a toddler or a teenager will challenge you on this point. Why should I do it your way? And sometimes you will question yourself, 'Do I have the right to insist on this?' I believe that unless a parent is willing to meet the right and wrong question head on, and be clear and convinced about the answer he/she will find raising children very hard work indeed. Raising children has more to do with these questions ultimately than it has to do with potty-training and choosing a school.

Not everyone would agree with me. Some people would like to do away with the categories of right and wrong altogether. They would argue that such categories are arbitrary and discouraging. This is precisely the issue behind some of the self-esteem mythology we discussed in the last chapter. After all while we all like ticks in our exercise books we don't like crosses. Let us just affirm everybody; let us assume that everybody is right.

But no one lives without moral categories. Even those who don't agree with the categories actually use them, although the terminology may be different.

## Three common ways of defining right and wrong

### 1. Naturalism

The argument of naturalism says that what is natural is good and right and what is unnatural is bad and wrong. It comes out of Darwinism and the idea of the survival of the fittest. It is natural to eat when you are hungry so it is right to do so. It is natural for children to play so they should be allowed and encouraged to do so. But can one get a moral code entirely from what is natural? I think not: after all, some things that are natural are unhelpful. It is natural for a baby with eczema to want to scratch herself but a wise parent will take steps to make sure she can't. It is natural for a child to want to explore but a wise parent will not let a child explore the motorway. It might be natural for a child to beat off physically another child who wants the toy he has, but that does not make it right. It does not take much thought to see that this is a hopeless way of proceeding. There are those 'modern' parents who will argue that sexual experimentation is natural for an adolescent and will therefore affect to be very relaxed about it. But any parent with half a brain knows that there are problems with just allowing nature to take its course. After all in nature, the weak, stupid and disabled die and the rest survive. Are we happy to apply that to the bringing up of children?

Some parents do try to go along the naturalism route in raising children: they are very chilled; they go with the flow but sooner or later they will find themselves setting some kind of arbitrary boundary—or they will resign themselves to private grief and disappointment—or they will die of exhaustion, trampled underfoot by the monster they have raised.

Those who have dabbled in the study of ethics may have come across the naturalistic fallacy. The mantra is: you can't get an 'ought' from 'is'. In other words, it is impossible to set up a moral code just from observing the way things happen in the world.

## 2. Happiness

Another common way of deciding right and wrong is on the basis of what makes you feel happy. 'If it feels right, do it.' 'Whatever turns you on.' These are the catchphrases of this philosophy. Moralists will often say that a side-effect of doing the right thing is the pleasure of doing it. So the person who does a good deed, e.g. helping a blind person to cross the road, can get quite a buzz from that act of kindness. But can you turn that round and say because it makes me happy it is the right way to go. Or, that anything that gives me a buzz is by definition right? Is your personal happiness an infallible guide when it comes to choosing a course of action?

Although it is a Biblical observation to point out that those who choose to do right are happy (e.g. Psalm 1; Proverbs 11:25), the Bible never offers happiness as a measure of the rightness of an action. We might try and argue this with our children (pointing out that being obedient will make them happy) but a recalcitrant teenager will find flaws in the argument. A teenager may be sublimely happy to stay under the duvet all day and not get up to go to school. A typical parental response would be that their personal happiness is irrelevant at that point; they have to do some things that are unpleasant in this life. Now some would argue that you could make the case for long-term happiness via success in exams and future job prospects. It might work. But if your son said, 'But actually I like slobbing around; money doesn't make me happy; my going to school and passing exams might make you happy but it doesn't float my boat,' how will you argue your case? You have not a leg to stand on.

The problem with using personal happiness as your guide in raising children is that you are raising someone to be totally self-absorbed. Because no man is an island, sooner or later your personal happiness will conflict with mine. To take a shocking example when a woman has her pregnancy terminated because her happiness is seriously at stake, one could ask what about the happiness of the individual whose life was ended? Or take the example of the person who puts his feet up on the opposite seat of a railway carriage. It makes him sublimely happy to relax in this way all the way from Waterloo to West Byfleet. But it has seriously compromised the happiness of the person who gets on at West Byfleet and finds the only seat available is filthy. You can make a moral code based on your personal happiness but it is likely at some point to make you unpopular or even get you in trouble with the police. And if you bring your children up that way you will always be wringing your hands apologetically as they complain about the 'injustice' of being made to be unhappy or bored for five seconds, or, you will be prison-visiting.

## 3. Consensus
Now some people see the flaws in all of the above and agree that

individual happiness cannot call the shots on right and wrong because logically individuals are going to come into conflict when their tastes and opinions differ. So they argue for a consensus on right and wrong. They say that when the majority of sane and sensible people agree on an issue then that makes it right. They argue that the universal laws protecting human life or property have come about that way. This is akin to John Stuart Mill's utilitarianism—the greatest happiness to the greatest number. So when a child complains about the 'unfairness' of bedtime at 7.30, a parent can talk about the expertise of people who have brought up children all over the world, plus the knowledge of slightly older people who have experienced how lack of sleep is detrimental to personal happiness and you can say therefore that it is right that the ordained bedtime is observed. You can use, as your consensus basis, government guidelines, the law of the land, the views of experts, the statistics printed in the newspaper, or the opinion of your friends. The teenage years again will throw up a problem. Because your teenager will also have a consensus group who all think that maybe getting legless is the greatest possible fun. They will tell you just everybody is going out dressed like this, so it must be right. Get with the beat.

Consensus can be informative, useful and helpful but it will not stand alone. Another stark example to point up its flaws: in 1950s America a young white girl was raped in an Alabama town. A vigilante mob came out and rounded up a random black youth and hanged him from the nearest tree. Everybody is agreed this is the right thing to do. It brought the most ecstatic happiness to the greatest number. But was it right? Does the fact that everybody thinks a certain thing necessarily make it right?

So you see our title asks a really important question. Right and wrong—who says? It can be extremely dangerous to say 'good is what I decide, or what other people decide it shall be.' In the book of Proverbs in the Bible we read 'There is a way that seems right to a man, but its end is the way to death' (Proverbs 14:12). But in Psalms, King David wrote: 'This God—his way is perfect; the word of the Lord proves true' (Psalm 18:30).

All that is saying that the most wise and sensible human being has a limited framework and is eminently capable of getting it wrong. We see what we see and there is plenty that we don't. A classic example of this is when you are sure that your child is lying but she sticks to her story. Where do you go from there? Such instances make us see how very unlikely we are to execute justice perfectly. What you need is the view from outside: the bird's-eye view, the Google map, the Satnav.

That is only to be found in the Bible. The wisdom of the Bible is the wisdom of the one 'Who has established all the ends of the earth' (Proverbs 30:4).

## The Biblical framework for morality and authority

### 1. God is the ultimate law-giver (Exodus 20; Deuteronomy 5)

God exists outside ourselves and sets the rules. God defines right and wrong according to his person. He is holy, the righteous one, the law-giver and the judge. He has the right because he is the creator of us and everything else. He holds every human being accountable for their actions and their failure to meet his standards.

## 2. Mankind is made in God's image

Mankind has been created to reflect God. In Genesis God says 'Let us make man in our image' (Genesis 1:26), and this distinguishes man from all the other living things God made. It is because we are made to reflect God that every human creature has this moral sense. That is why murder is universally considered wrong, and genocide, and rape and stealing and lying. There really is no other explanation for that

## 3. The effect of the fall

When Adam and Eve ignored God's prohibition and chose instead to go after being gods themselves, a fault-line was introduced into human nature. We need help and guidance morally because we are flawed in our thinking. In other words, although we all have a strong sense of right and wrong, it is not perfect. Not only so, we are capable of holding firmly to a moral principle like always telling the truth or behaving with kindness, but we don't do it. We do not practise what we preach. That failure is due to a persistent inbuilt bias to please ourselves instead of trusting God and letting him rule our lives. The human race has declared unilateral independence. And that is why the world is in a mess. Even the best of consciences needs help.

## 4. A parent's job description

Parents are there to direct their children (Exodus 20:12). Parents are not perfect but they are God's way of children being raised in a loving and safe environment. This is God's social service and he has given you a position of authority with regard to your children. So as God is the authority to whom you must answer, you are the authority to whom your children must answer. It is a delegated authority for the protection, direction, instruction and correction of your children. You do this because you love them. So the question right and wrong—who says so?—can be answered within the home by the parent: 'I say so.' You are there to train their consciences, teach them right from wrong, set boundaries, and correct your children when those boundaries are crossed. You are right to be firm. And you will answer to God for how you do this. That is why you need help: because it can be tough.

## 5. Law and grace

The Bible is more about grace than it is about law. Some people think the Bible is a set of rules, a moral standard. But that is not the case. The Bible certainly tells of a holy God; it certainly contains within it commandments about the best way to live—the maker's instructions. But the Bible is a story of a God who loved his chosen and wayward children so much, that he came himself to keep the law when they could not; to keep it for them, so that by trust him in him they would not be condemned (as they deserve to be) but rescued and after death be received into God's special country where there is nothing foul or corrupt. That is grace—God's kindness to rebellious men and women and boys and girls who put their hands up and say 'I'm messing up here, please rescue me.' So as parents we mess up and we need God's forgiveness. And when our children mess up, God's kindness to us enables us to be patient and gentle, even when we correct and instruct. So we are not cold-hearted and cruel, waving a big stick at our children; we delight in a relationship with our children (as God does with us) and in the context of that warm relationship we direct and correct our children and they receive it. This will come through again and again in this book, but the truth bears repeating that firmness in the context of a warm relationship is the only effective way to raise children who will not only be well-behaved but also, incidentally, happy.

To summarise the argument of this chapter, a secular worldview gives you no basis for absolute right and wrong. Of course we all know atheists who use these concepts but they are merely free-loading from a Christian heritage. Ultimately their 'right and wrong' will bear no challenge because they are without foundation. A Christian worldview, on the other hand, clarifies the issues perfectly. The moral standards of the Bible are clear, sensible and indefatigable.

## How the Christian worldview helps parents

### 1. The moral framework

A Christian worldview will enable you to maintain a moral framework in discipline. The question you ask yourself and you ask your child is 'Is this right or wrong?' So you will have no need to resort to bribery which is a mere arbitrary and quite cynical manipulation of variables to get the desired end-product. Instead, you will be confident to say, 'Don't do that; it is wrong', and, 'Do this; it is right'. You will know that your child, as a moral being, has this inbuilt friend inside, known as the conscience. And you will use that friend and train it to be your child's invaluable moral guide.

### 2. Clarity of aim

A Christian worldview will help you to work out the kind of child you want to raise. When you consider the question of what is important in raising a child you will see that the Bible's priorities are not in the direction of beauty, riches, success or fame. Instead you will have an eternal perspective which will give you a definite basis for wanting your child to be godly not worldly and for commending the kind of exquisite virtues which even sound old-fashioned today: honesty, modesty, unselfishness, chastity, humility, sportsmanship, loyalty and industry (to name but a few).

### 3. God's view of things

A brief glance at the kings of Old Testament Israel and Judah gives an important perspective. You always get a comment on their character 'in the sight of God'. Sometimes that is pretty much all the information you do get, as though that is all the reader needs to know. The writers are saying that to do 'evil in the eyes of the Lord' is the defining aspect of any given king's character and what happens after that will be along the lines of provoking the Lord to anger.

For today's parent dealing with peer pressure, celebrity culture and rampant materialism this is a needful corrective. We need to be continually reminded that it is not what people think, it is what God thinks that counts. It is not impressing people with the smart clothes, the right labels and the impeccable CV, it is character that is crucial. So you are not merely saying, as many money-lovers do, 'Money can't buy you happiness or health or love', you will want to discover and introduce your child to the extraordinary riches of knowing Jesus Christ. You will want to walk through life with him at your side, your rock in times of trouble, your guide in times of crisis, your Saviour at times of personal failure, your companion in the best of times and your comforter in the worst, and the only way to heaven. This is another level of living. Jesus said, 'I came that they may have life and have it abundantly' (John 10:10).

## 4. Honesty

The Christian worldview enables parents to examine themselves and be honest about failure. So many parents are troubled by guilt, some real guilt, some false or even imagined. And parental guilt can lead to inappropriate compensation which in turn can make a child manipulative, knowing precisely which buttons to press. But there is a better way than being continually surrounded by a murky cloud of unspecified guilt: face it in the light of the Bible's truth; sort out the real from the false. The Bible is clear that no parent gets it right all the time. But it is equally clear that there is always hope for the person who admits a mistake, when that admission leads them in repentance to seek God. (Hosea 5:15).

So, instead of pretending to be perfect (which fools no one, least of all a teenager) or curling up in a corner in self-loathing at your failure, take the Bible's path. Come to God and ask forgiveness. The grace of God is extraordinary and you will want to model to your children not only an adherence to God's law but a wonder at his grace. Our moral bankruptcy is dealt with by the death of Jesus, who took our punishment. And when Jesus is the director of your life, the question 'Right and wrong—who says so?' has an answer: he does.

## Some practical inferences and applications

1. Review the language you use when speaking to your children, especially in a discipline context. Do the words 'right' and 'wrong' make regular appearances? Perhaps you could bring them into all kinds of discussions to make them familiar concepts, which the children themselves will begin to internalise.

2. Work on developing discernment in your children. Proverbs 2 points out the many blessings of this. (See verses 9–11) One way to do this is through the medium of story. Stories enable the readers/listeners to enter a parallel world and to observe behaviour. Within that framework there is great scope for moral education as you discuss what the protagonist should do/ should have done and what are the likely consequences. This kind of discussion can equally be an outcome of watching films or TV together.

## For further reading

'Christians in a PC world' by John Benton (Evangelical Press)

# Chapter 4

# Delighting in our children

## As our heavenly Father delights in us

*'... and my parents finally realise that I'm kidnapped and they snap into action immediately: they rent out my room.'* Woody Allen

There is a bizarre ambivalence about contemporary parental attitude to their children. On the one hand they indulge them, organise their lives around them and fight to get them into the best schools and universities. On the other there is this understanding between parents as they roll their eyes and shrug their shoulders at each other that children are a bit of a bind, hard work and an obstacle to fun. Perhaps that is why the Americans invented summer camp. Certainly the sense that modern parents have that they must always be entertaining or educating their children has taken its toll.

But parents of an earlier generation did not necessarily get it right either. The poet Philip Larkin (born in 1922) was famously rude about his parents' input into his life, enshrining in verse the way his parents messed him up (although he used a less polite verb). According to Larkin's biographer, Andrew Motion, his father 'worked all day and shut himself away reading in the evening, or else gardening.'

When a parent has provided and protected, trained, instructed and corrected, has he completed the work of a parent? The stereotypical Victorian Papa, who shut himself in his library and emerged only to pat his children on the head, to preside over the meal table and family prayers and to administer the rod of correction as required, might be considered by some to be a kind of Christian role model, but a closer examination of Scripture will show that to be well short of the mark.

Our model for parenting is not history or tradition, or our own parents or friends or newspaper articles or parenting experts or government guidelines: our model is Almighty God, the Eternal Father. What can we learn there?

## The Trinitarian God

At the very heart of Christian theology is the concept of the fatherhood of God. It comes through the doctrine of the Trinity in which we understand God as the eternal Father of the eternal Son. *'I am the way, and the truth, and the life. No one comes to the Father except through me.'* John 14:6

John 14:6 tells us that Jesus is the only way to God, but also that the way to know God is as a Father. The God Jesus reveals is a fatherly God. So fatherhood is not a human idea which then, as some psychologists would have it, became enlarged in our imaginations until we invented a god to make us feel more secure. On the contrary, the whole notion of fatherhood comes from God as revealed in Scripture.

Here is how the doctrine of Trinity is really crucial to our ultimate model of fatherhood. If the Bible taught a mere single-person God, like, say, Allah, we could not know God in a loving relational way. We would be in awe of him; we might accept his sovereign rule and his right to admonish and discipline us. In fact he would be like the ultimate Victorian papa. But would we dare ask him anything? Wouldn't we rather be constantly aware that, apart from our sins, we were a rather annoying distraction, getting on his nerves?

But this is not the God revealed in Scripture, though some have pretended so or have deliberately misunderstood. Yes, God is awesome but he is a loving Father who sovereignly cares for his family. The Father has always poured out his love on his Son (John 17:26) and his aim in sending Jesus on that rescue mission was so that Jesus would be the firstborn among many brothers (Roman 8:29) and bring many sons to glory. (Hebrews 2:10).

## The Fatherhood of God

A father begets children, giving them life and love. So believers are described as being born again into his family to become his children (John 1:12). The apostle Paul uses the language of being adopted into God's family (Ephesians 1:5). As God's children we are also heirs and there is not only a home (John 14:2) but a wonderful inheritance awaiting us (Ephesians 1:14).

This is a huge study and worthy of whole book of its own. But suffice it to say that knowing God through his Son as a father is not only immensely comforting to our souls (and that is an understatement) but is also a matchless model to us of what a father should be and do. Of course, in a fallen world we cannot measure up but at least we can understand the shape of what should be and the direction in which we should be moving as parents.

Before we go on to look at our own parenting after the pattern of God the Father, let us look at some specific actions of the Father God via a brief sample of explicit paternal Scripture texts.

### 1. Sustained commitment

Moses reminds the children of Israel on the brink of the promised land that the story of their journey is not only of God's provision of direction, but one of God picking them up and carrying them to their destination, just like a father with a weary or recalcitrant child.

'... you have seen how the Lord your God carried you, as a man carries his son, all the way that you went until you came to this place.' Deuteronomy 1:31

Isaiah takes up a similar theme when talking to wayward Judah. He reminds them of the kind of God they have.

'Listen to me, O house of Jacob,
all the remnant of the house of Israel,
who have been borne by me from before your birth,
carried from the womb;
even to your old age I am he,
and to grey hairs I will carry you.
I have made, and I will bear;
I will carry and will save.'                          Isaiah 46:3–4

## 2. Gracious reception and protection

The history of God and his people is one of not of give and take but of give and give, on God the Father's part. His children disobey, refuse to heed his warnings and get into a frightful mess all of their own making. And yet the loving Father receives his wayward children back. This is the promise to Judah, about to be taken into captivity to Babylon because of their wilful idolatry:

'With weeping they shall come,
and with pleas for mercy I will lead them back,
I will make them walk by brooks of water,
in a straight path in which they shall not stumble,
for I am a father to Israel,
and Ephraim is my firstborn.'                          Jeremiah 31:9

The same idea is used in Jesus' famous parable of the lost son. The father, exploited and spurned, waits and watches for the return of his wayward son and runs to meet him, welcoming him home with joy (Luke 15:20).

### 3. Knowledge and compassion

God the Father knows precisely what his children are made of. He is also well aware of their vulnerability and weakness. And this draws out of him, not exasperation, but compassion.

> 'As a father shows compassion to his children,
> so the Lord shows compassion to those who fear him.
> For he knows our frame;
> he remembers that we are dust.'                    Psalm 103:13–14

Jesus takes up the theme of the father heart of God in the Sermon on the Mount. God our Father not only knows us, he knows what we need and undertakes to provide. This is the complete antidote to worry: trust in the Father God. A child need not worry whether or not there will be breakfast tomorrow because she knows that someone is taking care of such things.

> 'For the Gentiles seek after all these things, and your heavenly Father knows that you need them all.'                    Matthew 6:32

### 4. Teaching, nurturing, healing

Calvin, writing in the Institutes on the providence of God, says that that the point of it all is that God's children should be under his protection to be nourished and educated. It is not a cold, distant providence, but a loving, concerned one. Hosea writes of this aspect of God's fatherhood.

> 'When Israel was a child, I loved him,
> and out of Egypt I called my son.
> The more they were called,
> the more they went away;

they kept sacrificing to the Baals
and burning offerings to idols.

   Yet it was I who taught Ephraim to walk;
I took them up by their arms,
but they did not know that I healed them.
I led them with cords of kindness,
with the bands of love,
and I became to them as one who eases the yoke on their jaws,
and I bent down to them and fed them.'      Hosea 11:1–4

## 5. Disciplining

The God who is a father is careful to discipline. Although this discipline is retributive, it is also restorative in purpose, wanting to shape character.

   '[Our fathers] disciplined us for a short time as it seemed best to them, but [God] disciplines us for our good, that we may share his holiness.'      Hebrews 12:10

## 6. Giving, forgiving, rewarding

God loves to give his children gifts; he loves to respond to their requests and often exceeds their desires.

   'If you then, who are evil, know how to give good gifts to your children, how much more will your Father who is in heaven give good things to those who ask him!'      Matthew 7:11

God is also ready to forgive those who ask his forgiveness. He particularly wants his children to be totally sincere not merely putting on a show to impress others. Such genuine behaviour

towards him will be rewarded. God is always more interested in
the inside than the outside.

> '... your Father who sees in secret will reward you.'
>
> Matthew 6:4, 6 and 18.

In fact the whole of the Sermon on the Mount (Matthew 5–7)
could be looked upon as a treatise on the fatherhood of God
and his relationship with and expectations of his children. Jesus
describes God as Father more there than in any other discourse
except the farewell discourse of John 14–16.

A key verse in the sermon, when Jesus is contrasting God's way
of doing things with the traditions of men, is:

> 'You therefore must be perfect, as your heavenly Father is perfect.'
>
> Matthew 5:48

God is our role model, our pattern our standard. In particular
he is referred to as our heavenly Father when we are called to
imitate him. He sets the standard for his children in love and
sincerity and generosity and service and forgiveness. He wants
them to be like him, following his example, aspiring to his ways.
He also sets the standard in fatherhood.

## The delight of God

The delight of God the Father is his Son (Matthew 3:17). As
we are in Christ, God is more than ready to delight in us with a
fatherly delight. Even where he disciplines, there is a throbbing
heart of love behind it.

"'Is Ephraim my dear son?
Is he my darling child?
For as often as I speak against him,
I do remember him still.
Therefore my heart yearns for him;
I will surely have mercy on him",
declares the Lord.'                                    Jeremiah 31:20

This is the amazing verb: God doesn't simply tolerate his children, he delights in them. He is entranced. I remember with each of my four children, how in the days following the birth, exhausted and sore as I was, I would put my head on my pillow for a rest and smile to picture that little face. My heart exulted. When my grown up children turn up on my doorstep I experience the same thrill. They are not perfect, they have caused me a deal of hard work over the years, but I delight in them. I love their presence.

That is a minute reflection of God's delight in us and all the more amazing because he is not a sinner dealing with another sinner, but dwells in glorious holiness and still welcomes, in Christ, a mucky loser like me.

The prophet Zephaniah paints a picture of a powerful warrior God who likes nothing better than to cuddle and soothe his troubled children, singing over them songs of joy and comfort.

'The Lord your God is with you,
the Mighty Warrior who saves.
He will take great delight in you;

in his love he will no longer rebuke you,
but will rejoice over you with singing.'                    Zephaniah 3:17

Finally, consider the goal of the gospel. Did God save us just because he could, to prove a point and score one over Satan? Was it a cold and clinical affair just to set the universe straight? Was God hoping for an army of little minions to do his bidding? Not at all. God sent Jesus to die so that we could be restored to relationship with him. Not only at peace with him so that there is a lasting truce but actually to enjoy contact and communication and the presence of each other. Paul writes to the Thessalonians and reminds them that this is the whole point:

'Our Lord Jesus Christ who died for us so that whether we are awake or asleep *we might live with him.*'
1 Thessalonians 5:10 (Emphasis mine)

The restored relationship with God is not a mere by-product of the gospel. 'Oh, by the way, you have a free pass into God's presence now, should you need it.' It is the point. That relationship was ruined in Eden when Satan insinuated to Adam and Eve that God was only interested in their keeping of the rule and didn't give a fig-leaf about their future happiness. At immense cost, God gave his Son so that sinners could be brought back into the bosom of the family with all that means. In particular that means a close relationship with the Father who loves us quite unreasonably to bits. And he wants us to be with him.

## God's fatherhood and our parenting
So having tried to distil the essence of God's fatherhood, which is

love and a massive personal delight in his ransomed children, let us apply it to our own work of parenting.

We can see from the above that as parents who give life to our children, the fundamental thing we also must give is love. It is love which lies behind all that patient nurturing, feeding, protecting, providing and training. We want to be the very best of role models for our children and we are concerned for their character development not just external appearances. We will take trouble to know our children and understand their needs.

Here are some things that Biblical parenthood, after God the Father's pattern, is not:

- It is not mere sentimentality. Hugs and kisses are great but children need something deeper.

- It is not sheer indulgence. God knows our needs but he does not acquiesce to our whims. Sometimes in his wisdom he makes us wait for what he intends to give us. So to be a parent after God's pattern will mean sometimes saying 'yes' and sometimes 'no' and sometimes 'wait'. This last is very helpful in the training of a child.

- It is not always intense. God's desire that we should be with him is sometimes just a resting in his presence, not continual badgering. I am thinking of Psalm 131 where David says he has stilled and quietened his soul like a weaned child with its mother. A weaned child is happy to have his mother around but not always clawing at her. While the relationship is still of supreme importance there is also room for a certain independence. So your relationship with your children may be one of comfortable being around each other in a warm and easy-going way. You do not always have to be interacting, interrogating, or tutoring. You just enjoy being with them.

- It is not about stuff. Although God gives us gifts, the greatest and most significant gift is that of himself, by the Holy Spirit. We love to give our children gifts and it is not wrong to do so. But don't do it too much. We see the giving of gifts as an expression of our love and because we think that the things we buy will make them happy. Many parents acknowledge helplessly that their children have far too many toys. Buy less. The greatest gift you give to your children is yourself. They want a relationship with you.

## Ways to delight in your children

### 1. Common ground

Find activities that you can enjoy together. Relationships thrive on frequent injections of chilling out together. It might be through playing football or snakes and ladders; it might be through a film or TV programme or a story that you can relish side by side and which forms the subject of further conversation; it might be through some shared activity or adventure.

### 2. Common meals

Eat together. This is very Biblical: the Bible is packed with significant shared meals because a shared meal is significant. It signifies acceptance and belonging. That is why the Pharisees made such a fuss about Jesus eating with tax collectors and sinners. It is also a non-threatening together time. Resist the temptation to put a trough in front of your children and walk away. God doesn't do that with us. Jesus knocks at the door and wants to be invited to eat with us and us with him. (Revelation 3:20). The meal table is great place to check in with each other, share news and stories and jokes and songs or just to be together in the middle of a busy schedule.

## 3. Common history

The shared history is very important to God's people in Scripture. In the Psalms God's dealings with his people are oft-repeated. As a source of praise and reassurance they also are an identifying mark, saying 'this is us'. Family photograph albums work well in this regard. Ours was so often fingered that it fell to pieces. But more important is the album you are creating in your child's heart and in your own. Build a bank of memories. You can do this through your own unique family routines: the things that you do regularly in the way you do them. This might be seasonal routines like walking through bluebells, or decorating a Christmas tree or building a bonfire; it might be daily ones like storytime or bathtime or songs or prayers that you share. Create these, work at them, revisit them and recall them with joy.

## Relationship strengtheners

### 1. Let them help

God lets us serve him. He doesn't need us at all to get done what he wants to get done. In one sense he could do it much better without us. But he has graciously prepared good works for us to do (Ephesians 2:10). He has given each of us gifts and knows that it is best for us if we use them and improve them in his service. So, even when it would be easier, quicker and more effective to perform tasks by yourself, occasionally let your children help. Encourage them to do so. Stir up their gifts or give them a chance to uncover new ones. Most of all let them find joy in unselfish acts. That is excellent training.

## 2. Let them speak

God enjoys hearing from us, even when he knows what we intend to say (Matthew 7:7). So take time to listen to your children and understand them better. Learn not only what they need and what they like but also what they fear and what they dream of; always keep the door of communication open. Make the most of a car journey, when you are giving your teenager a lift somewhere, to listen, not just for what he says, but also for the heart message. Ask them sometimes what they think about things. Give an opportunity as they grow for them sometimes to have input into some family decision-making.

## 3. Let them listen

The way we know God is through his word. From the earliest age teach your children to listen and enjoy listening to what you have to say. I will major on teaching them to listen to commands in a later chapter, but actually they are much more likely to look you in the eyes and listen to an instruction if they are already familiar and comfortable with you talking in other modes. The Bible is full of stories. God knows how important they are to the human psyche. So be like God in this too. Tell them stories. And I mean tell, not just read, though reading is good. But telling, eyeball to eyeball is making a world between you just with words and inviting the child to come and play with you in it. So try telling a Bible story, or a story from your own childhood with your eyes wide and your speech animated and see how you can capture a child audience. There are other sorts of telling as well: instruction about life skills and attitudes are the business of a parent. See the book of Proverbs for examples. If delivered with a light and warm touch all the better. Telling is not telling off.

## Relationship busters

### 1. Lying

There is really no answer to lying; it truly does bust relationships because without truth communication can't happen. One should distinguish between imaginative story telling which can be part of the language and conceptual development of a young child and the deliberate falsehoods told by a child usually to cover another offence. God hates lying: in his list of things which are an abomination to him in Proverbs 6:16–19 lying comes up twice. Teach your children those verses. Punishments should be mitigated when the truth is told. But ultimately if you are sure your child is lying but you have no proof and she won't give way, there is nothing you can do but shake your head sadly and remind the culprit that God sees what is done in secret. On the positive side teach your children the liberation of eyeball to eyeball honesty. Let them discover what a wonderful relief it is to just own up. Show them David's experience in Psalm 32. When he kept silent, he suffered in many ways; but when he confessed he knew the release of forgiveness. Truthfulness is a beautiful thing as all God's attributes are and should be promoted and celebrated as such.

### 2. Bad behaviour

This is true for God and us. Our sins separate us from God. Our children's sins make a distance between them and us. As those who have trusted Christ it is impossible that even our sins would make God cast us off for ever, but they do grieve the Holy Spirit and something is definitely lost in the relationship until we are made to face up to our sins and there is contrition and confession. Sometimes God has to discipline us in some way to bring that about. That is another reason why discipline is so important. Unchecked or ignored misbehaviour can do long-term damage to a relationship. There is little pleasure in being with a rude and uncooperative child. Your child's challenging behaviour spoils the time you spend together. So confront it, correct or punish it as appropriate and then restore the relationship to normality.

### 3. Disappointment

Sometimes we are disappointed with our children. They let us down and sometimes their misbehaviour hurts and we think to ourselves about such a child : 'I love you to pieces but I don't like you much.' This is where compassion comes into play. God knows our frame and remembers we are dust (Psalm 103:14) Our children are growing and developing and while they are doing so they make a lot of mistakes. At such times it is also salutary to remember how very wayward and unlovely we have been as God's children and yet he has received us back again and again. We are still welcome in his house. He remains committed to us and keeps working on us. Forgive as the Lord forgave you.

### 4. Favouritism

Jacob had twelve sons but he loved Joseph best and he showed it (Genesis 37:3). This in no way exonerates Joseph's brothers from the thuggery they practised on him, but it did give them ammunition for their entirely unmerited hatred of him and it was a serious error by Jacob. Joseph's brothers were for the most part hard, rough, unprincipled men and Jacob had done very little about it except complain that it put him in a difficult position (Genesis 44:30). But this unlove on the part of Jacob no doubt had a long history and you can't do much with children if they think you dislike them. Beware of favouritism if you have multiple children. Your children are all different. Don't expect them to be the same and don't compare them to each other. Each one is uniquely made by God with different gifts. That is God's way, to gift differently so that each person brings something unique and special to the mix (See 1 Corinthians 12 to see how this applies in the church.) It applies equally in the family. Recognise and enjoy your children's differences.

## 5. Rivalry

This follows on from the last point and it is what happens if a child perceives or believes that he is less loved than a sibling. If it is a true perception then I refer the parent to the above paragraph. That is completely wrong. But more commonly it is a false perception based on insecurity. And it comes out most distastefully in bickering and sniping and the malicious telling of tales. What can a parent do? First of all, explicitly celebrate the differing gifts of your children. Let them each understand what an asset it is to have this brother or sister with his or her unique gifts and personality on the team. Make sure that each child's gifts are recognised and given opportunity for use and display. Sometimes squabbling children should be left to sort themselves out. Don't intervene too quickly. Turn up the radio or do the hoovering and, provided there is no danger to life or limb, let them discover for themselves strategies for harmonious co-existence.

Meanwhile work at the other end of the problem. Make time

for each of your children individually. It may only be a short time, say at the end of the day, when you have a one-to-one before bedtime, or with an older sibling after the younger has gone to bed. Or it may be an occasional Saturday afternoon when a parent engages with just one of the children at a time. In one family I know, the father has taken each of the children, separately, on a weekend camping trip. Every time it turned out to be a real bond-strengthener. The children discover in this kind of way that they are valued for themselves and they have the opportunity to get to know their parent better. God the Father loves and values us individually but he does expect us to function cooperatively in the local church. This is the expectation of family life too.

## A reciprocal relationship

In the Bible, no less than God delights in us, so we his children are encouraged to delight in him.

> 'Delight yourself in the Lord,
> and he will give you the desires of your heart.'          Psalm 37:4

As erring and very flawed parents we do not, indeed could not, demand that from our children as a right. But the extraordinary thing is that it happens and is a sign of the exquisite nature of the parent/child relationship at its best.

> 'Grandchildren are the crown of the aged,
> and the glory of children is their fathers.'          Proverbs 17:6

A memorable illustration of this is in the 1967 film of E. Nesbit's 'The Railway Children'. It is a scene which makes grown men cry. The occasion is the return of the children's falsely imprisoned father to the family. He arrives on the station where Bobby, the eldest daughter, gradually recognises him through billowing clouds of steam. This is how E. Nesbit wrote it:

'Only three people got out of the 11.54. The first was a countrywoman with two baskety boxes full of live chickens who stuck their russet heads out anxiously through the wicker bars; the second was Miss Peckitt, the grocer's wife's cousin, with a tin box and three brown-paper parcels; and the third—

'Oh! My Daddy, my Daddy!' That scream went like a knife into the heart of everyone in the train, and people put their heads out of windows to see a tall pale man with lips set in a thin close line, and a little girl clinging to him with arms and legs, while his arms went tightly round her.'

## Some practical inferences and applications

1. How does God's fatherhood help you to see your way as a parent? Which fatherly activity of God have you as a parent been least inclined to imitate?

2. How are you demonstrating to your children your delight in them? Review your children's present needs and interests and see whether you could use one of the relationship-strengthener ideas mentioned in this chapter.

# Chapter 5

# The wonderful concept of obedience

## Biblical parenting is both simple and beautiful

*A GP was trying to listen attentively to a mother describing the symptoms of the 3 month old baby in her arms. The baby's 3-year old brother meanwhile amused himself by whizzing himself round and round in the doctor's chair. It was a noisy and distracting activity. The mother rolled her eyes at the doctor with a 'what-can-you-do?' expression. The doctor decided to be proactive since the mother apparently was helpless. He stopped the spinning of the chair by holding it firmly and looked the 3-year old in the eyes. He said, 'Now I need to listen and talk to your mother about your baby sister. So you sit still and quiet for a few minutes.' The child stared at the doctor in wide-eyed astonishment. Stunned by the firm tone of voice he complied with the instruction. The doctor completed the consultation without further interruption. As the mother left with her children she said to the doctor, 'That was amazing. Would you like to come and babysit at our house some time?'*

*'Most parents these days are at the mercy of their children.' That is the observation of the Christian GP who told me the above story. Many primary school teachers would agree. It is not just that parents are afraid to confront and correct; many dismiss the possibility of obedience as an unrealistic aim. The best most of them attempt is a kind of jollying along and hoping their children don't let them down too much in front of their friends. In running parenting courses I have met parents for whom the setting of boundaries is a completely novel idea. Such parents are completely rudderless, adrift on a sea of mostly unproven ideas, picked up from newspapers, TV or friends.*

## The framework

The best-selling book by Pamela Druckerman, 'French children don't throw food' talks about the importance of the 'cadre', the framework in which children are free to operate. This is wisdom but the book is a bit vague and whimsical about what actually this framework is.

The Bible, on the other hand, is quite clear: the framework is obedience. The child must obey his parents (Exodus 20:12;

Ephesians 6:1). This is to be the reasonable expectation of every parent of his offspring; not only reasonable, but also kind, for surely it is in the child's interest to obey without question or delay the parent's instruction. Such obedience might save a child's life on a busy road one day.

## Good for children

I had this paraphrase of Proverbs 29:15 written up, framed and hanging on the wall of our stairs at home:

> 'Correction and discipline are good for children; if a child has his own way he will make his mother ashamed of him.'

Because it is not generally pleasant to correct and discipline, and it is certainly not fashionable, I needed that reminder from God's word to encourage me as I led one of our four upstairs for a spot of correction.

Why has such sensible advice gone by the board? Apart from the falling out of favour of the whole notion of authority in the post-modern mindset, there is the view of the child. You treat a child according to what you think a child is.

It is a bit like when you pick up a pile of post from the mat behind your front door. At the briefest of glances you will assess the various items and on the basis of that assessment sort the post. Junk mail goes straight into the recycling; bills are put into a safe place to be dealt with later; but a personal, handwritten letter is greeted with a smile and savoured. So what do you think a child is? As you think of a child so you will treat him.

## Alternative views of children

### 1. Innocent or wayward?

Do you believe that your child, if allowed to have absolutely free, unfettered choice as to behaviour and attitude, without any input or direction from you, will turn into a delightful human being,— polite, hard-working, generous, affectionate? Some people think that. But does a child naturally share toys? Or does he clutch the best toy to his breast, even when he doesn't want to play with it, to prevent any other child using it?

Of course there is an innocence about children—they are weak and defenceless and need the benign protection of adults; there is also an innocence in the sense of ignorance. There is so much they don't know and they need the benign instruction of adults and the benign direction of adults. But here is a question to ponder: who has raised a child who has always done as you benignly directed him? Even when that direction was delivered kindly, calmly, clearly and in the best interests of everybody? Of course, no one! So it is clear, without opening the Bible, that there is a waywardness about every human being born into this world. It is evident to anyone who has ever stood in a playground and just watched. There is nothing innate in a child to make him choose the right thing to do automatically—a child is driven by what will gratify and please him now although he will be quick to point out the unfairness of other children who do just that. If you recognise this facet of children you will know that children need not only benign protection and direction and instruction, they also need benign correction.

That is what Proverbs 22:15 is getting at when it says:

'Folly is bound up in the heart of a child,
but the rod of discipline drives it far from him.'

## 2. A free spirit or under authority?

The concept of parental authority and the attempts to undermine it were discussed in chapter 1, but it must be mentioned again briefly because it is crucial to grasp it if you hope to train your child in obedience.

The children's rights lobby have done some good. They have raised awareness of abuse, cruelty and neglect of defenceless children. So far, so good. But they have also created a mindset which says that adults are the enemies of children. Parents are not to be trusted. The children's rights lobby has undermined the confidence of ordinary parents to exercise authority over children. And how can you instruct, direct or correct without authority? So, parents are asking these days, 'Do I have the right to say "no" here, or to insist that such and such a thing is done this way?' After all the child has rights and if she says she doesn't want to go to bed at 7 o'clock and I cannot convince her that it is for her own good, then perhaps I ought to let her stay up. Is it an affront to a child's dignity to insist that he does what his mother says? This is the kind of muddle we are in which has led to discipline in some circles being a dirty word.

The Bible is very helpful here. It ascribes immense dignity to a child because by a Bible worldview, every child born into the world is not a mere product of chance, but a living soul, made in the image of God. Therefore a child is worthy of the utmost respect. Jesus himself gave dire warnings to any who would take advantage of a child's defenceless state to harm a child. At the same time one of the Bible's big ideas is family: a child is born into a system of care. This care package is built into the Ten Commandments by the words, 'Honour your father and your mother that your days may be long in the land'. It is the recipe for a happy life that a child is to be under his parents' authority, obedient to them. This is benign authority, based purely on the fact that they are his parents, not because they are perfect or bigger or cleverer. They are his parents and therefore they have authority and should be free to exercise it in the child's interest. Not everyone believes that, but if you believe the Bible and know it to be God's infallible word, you can be confident in your authority.

### 3. Pal or pupil?

Some people want their children to be their friends. That is an understandable ambition. You the parent are unquestionably on your child's side. But that does not mean it is wise or appropriate, even if it were possible, to adopt the guise of a three year old along with your three year old. Some parents even drop the titles Mummy and Daddy in favour of first names. 'Call us Bob and Felicity,' they say. It is a statement of equality, of buddies together walking the road of life.

Of course, you want to have the very best relationship with your children. In fact I frequently stress that a warm relationship is an essential context for effective discipline. But not a buddy relationship. It is quite hard to correct your buddy. The Bible says that the child should obey the parent; the parent does not obey the child. Although there is an equality of value and dignity between parent and child, there is a difference in status during the growing years. You the parent are there to do a job. You love your child to bits but you are there to protect, instruct, direct and correct him. The boot is firmly on that foot. Gradually, during the teenage years authority metamorphoses into influence.

So don't apologise for being the grown-up. Your child needs you to be the grown-up. Your child is at his most sublimely secure when you are clearly and confidently calling the shots and setting the boundaries. And this is true even when he thinks you are being harsh or grim. Don't flinch. He'll get over it.

## Popular substitutes for discipline

Because discipline is unpopular and can be unpleasant we can find ourselves employing other techniques to manage our children. Here are some of the things parents find themselves doing instead of training in obedience.

1. Excuse them. This is the voice of therapy culture. Sometimes we make excuses for our child's misbehaviour. We say, 'he's tired, she's had a hard day, he's disappointed, she's traumatised, he's got low self-esteem ...' Now all of those things may be true. But that is not the point. The point is this: are we going to allow our children to take responsibility for their own behaviour/misbehaviour or not? Or is it always going to be the fault of someone else or of the circumstances? I am not saying we cannot be understanding or sympathetic. But if we are going to praise our children when they do well, surely it is logical to chastise them when they do badly. They make choices, which are moral choices, all day long. If we commend them for the good we cannot merely excuse the bad. That is very poor training because it teaches them to blame-shift.

2. Ignore them. This is the voice of liberalism, which would be inclined to allow the children as far as possible to do as they like. When called upon to intervene liberalism refuses to recognise an absolute moral worldview, whereby some things are definitely wrong and some things are definitely right. This is a failure in discipline because we need to instruct our children's sense of right and wrong and that this is quite outside of how they feel about it. It might feel great to pull someone's hair but it is wrong. Children have a moral sense, they have a conscience and this conscience is your friend when you discipline. Bring in right and wrong as absolutes. And be clear that the fundamental right course of action for a child is obedience to you.

3. Organise them—the voice of strategic management. Some parents work really hard to avoid the occasion for misbehaviour by organising their children's life and surroundings. You tie up the cupboards; you take the plug off the computer; you run a tight schedule. You make prevention of confrontation your responsibility. If your child misbehaves it is your fault for not organising the circumstances so that it was impossible for them to misbehave. By taking this approach you are denying your child the freedom to fail. But you are forgetting that in general in this life we learn more by getting things wrong than by getting things right. It is one of the great routes to wisdom: learn by your mistakes. A child has to have some independence in order to learn to take responsibility. They need to be let off the leash so that they will understand the need for self-discipline. Otherwise you are deceiving yourself. So back off occasionally and see what he/she does.

4. Consult them. This is where you always ask the child what he or she would like. There is a place for that of course, say, in a restaurant. But in many parents' vocabularies, the language of choice has replaced the language of command. They say, 'Would you like to wash your hands and come to the table?' Do they really mean that doing those things is optional and that the child can legitimately say 'no'? It is an habitual turn of phrase but it also carries a message. And it can turn into parental wheedling and coaxing a child when in fact perhaps she could have just kindly but firmly instructed. It sometimes seems that parents are afraid to tell their children what to do. I want to suggest that it is fine to just say what you want to happen and insist that it does. Parenting is not a consultation exercise. You are the adult and you are there to take the long view and decide what is best. You don't have to shout and rant, you can just say, 'This is what is happening now.' Be in charge.

5. Bribe them. It seems such a great idea and in the short-term can be extremely effective. And I am well aware that it is highly recommended in some circles. But it is a poor choice. Firstly because it does not change anything inside— being extrinsic, it only changes outward behaviour and that only just enough to hit off the reward. After that, normal misbehaviour can be and often is resumed. But worse than that, bribery takes behaviour out of the moral framework and makes obedience to you optional. Can that be right? What if the child turns down your proffered sweets or sticker and decides being disobedient is more fun? Do you enter into negotiations and up the ante? You are teaching the child that the only reason to comply is if there is something

(material) in it for him. But remember that the Bible says, 'Children obey your parents in the Lord, for this is right.' Certainly the next verse talks about the promise attached of a long life in the land. But that is only saying what I often told my children: 'Good boys are happy boys; good girls are happy girls.' As a Christian parent you will want your children ultimately to choose good behaviour for its own sake. If you habitually bribe them you are effectively denying the child the opportunity for finding out that good behaviour is its own reward.

Of course rewards are mentioned in the Bible, for example in the parable of the ten minas (Luke 19) but in that parable the reward is in the form of greater responsibility. The kind of rewards that Jesus talks about are not of this world. God even describes himself as a reward (Genesis 15:1) so rewards in the Bible are not really equivalent to a sticker or extra pocket money. As a recognition and reinforcement of past good behaviour or effort a parent might well reward a child. That is not bribery. Bribery is when a parent is trying to negotiate an outcome and manipulate the future.

Each of the above strategies fails to address the issue that here is someone who is at heart foolish and ignorant and who needs instruction and correction. Some of them may seem to be working really well and make your children look good, especially in public. But they are cosmetic. Your job as a parent is to train. Training takes time and demands your consistent attention. It is a process which may frequently seem arduous. Don't give up or be put off because outwardly your children may not look as well polished in public as the children who are bribed and organised.

Training in obedience is worth the hassle. If you are persistent and consistent in the pre-school years, you will reap the reward of children who are secure, pleasant and trustworthy. You will also be able to confidently permit them a good deal of liberty because you know that they are operating within that framework of obedience to you. And your home will be harmonious. There may still be skirmishes but the war is over.

## Your word is law

The thing you want your child to grasp is that when you speak, your words carry significance. They carry a particular significance because you are the parent. In a very small and pathetic way our parenting of our children is like God's parenting of us. He is not a silent parent but a speaking one. And the fact that he speaks to us is hugely significant and gracious. When he speaks we are supposed to take him seriously. His words to us are light and life. (Psalm 119:105). Similarly a parent's words to his children are intended to be a route to wisdom (Proverbs 4:1–13). So when you give your child an instruction, obedience is not optional, nor is it negotiable, any more than we can argue with Almighty God when he has told us what to do. When God speaks, something is supposed to happen. When you as a parent speak to your child in a tone of instruction you expect something to happen. And you will wait around to follow through and see that it does, commending compliance and reprimanding non-compliance.

One of the implications of grasping this is that perhaps you might give fewer instructions to your children. Don't just rattle them off into the air hoping against hope that some of them might be somewhat obeyed. Speak purposefully and resolutely. Then your child will learn that you expect obedience.

People often ask me when to start training in obedience. I would say the time to start is when you are confident that there is a clear two-way channel of verbal communication between you and your child; this will normally happen with most children around 2 years old, give or take 6 months either way. Up to that time discipline is imposed on your child via routines which you decide in the interests of the health and happiness of the child. You will also already be setting boundaries by the use of the word 'no' and you will be careful to ensure that if you have said 'no' to something, you follow through on a failure to comply either by removing the opportunity for mischief from the child or removing the child from the opportunity.

Discipline needs a context of good communication and warm relationship. Discipline does not happen in a vacuum, it works within everyday communication and relationship and if those are poor the discipline won't happen. But with both good communication and a loving relationship your child can learn obedience.

## Six steps in obedience training

1. Stop what you are doing and look at the child—the point here is that you are consciously training. You are not merely remarking to the world at large that it would be nice if something happened. So this demands your undivided attention. For obvious reasons therefore it is no good doing this when you are under pressure to get out of the house for an appointment.

2. Wait for the child to stop what he is doing and look at you. There is no point in speaking until you know that your child is

receiving you. Children are very good at selective deafness. This is one way you will signal to your child that you are about to say something important. You may have to get down to his level i.e. on the floor. What you want is eye contact—an essential component of communication. You are allowed to smile and be friendly.

3. Give the instruction once. If you say it twice she learns not to listen the first time. With a toddler it will be a simple instruction normally to do with fetching something, putting something away or going somewhere, e.g. 'Put your toys in the box.'

4. Ask the child what he is to do. The idea of that is to a) make absolutely certain that the child has got the message and b) to make her take ownership of the desired response. Don't stand for any nonsense at this point. That will usually be a cover for a challenge to your authority. When she answers correctly you can say 'Absolutely. Well done.'

5. Stand and wait. This is the hardest thing to do but it is essential to follow through on your instruction. You have spoken. You expect something to happen as a result. So resist the temptation to go off and make a cup of coffee or text a friend. Stay on the case, totally focused. Be an emphatic presence in the room.

6. Encourage, encourage, encourage. While you are standing and waiting, notice and respond positively to the slightest move in the right direction. Be explicit that more than you wanted the toys put away you wanted obedience and you are highly delighted when you get it.

I put the above as a six-part strategy because parents have told me that they find it helpful. But life is complicated, situations and children vary, and no parent will be able to always follow that pattern to the letter. However you will get the gist and adapt it to suit your own circumstances. The main point is the fact that your word carries weight and your child learns that it is essential to take notice of it. Consistency is the key in training.

## Some practical tips

- Develop a voice of command. I meet many delightful Christian parents who exhibit wonderful sweetness and gentleness. But when they are giving commands they need to find a teacher voice, a tone which says no-nonsense, not a 'would you mind awfully ...?' wheedle. Your children will then recognise that they need to get into obedience mode.

- Have realistic expectations and boundaries. I made the mistake many times myself, especially with our long-suffering eldest, of setting the bar too high. In doing so I made all our lives hard and everybody unhappy. He survived but I learned that in the interest of fairness and if I wanted any degree of success it was sensible to assess what was a realistic expectation of any of my children at a given age. Know your child.

- Be very clear about what you want to see. We usually know what we don't like. But it is helpful to think about what you actually want to see in any given situation. Not only is that a more positive perspective, if you explain it to the child it enables him to catch a vision of what obedience would look like at this point.

- Support the weak. It is undoubtedly true that there is vast individual difference in compliance. Some children seem to be born wanting to please their parents and are so sensitive to parental displeasure that they are fast learners in the obedience stakes. Others are wilful and resistant. Modelling the action you want done or helping with it might form part of the training, as might a pre-warning that an instruction is going to come in the next few minutes.

Over the years of running parenting courses the session on discipline is the one that draws the most concentrated attention. Generally in the question times I would say that 90% of the questions are connected with it.

## Common problems with discipline

### 1. No!

What do you do with the child who just will not comply? Recognise a challenge to your authority for what it is. It may be covered by joking, whining, or a refusal to engage. This has to be taken seriously and painful sanctions must be put in place. More on those in chapter 6. But realise that this is serious and you cannot let it go with a laugh or a shrug. If you have spoken, even if you regret having done so, you must not backtrack. That would only store up more problems later.

### 2. Ouch

Sometimes Christian parents ask whether they ought simply to forgive their children when they misbehave. I think this is to confuse two issues, namely the issue of training in obedience and the issue of the pain your child causes you when he disobeys.

Forgiveness has no part in the training in obedience. There is a sense in which training is quite dispassionate. There are times when you have to be completely inflexible to make your point. Your message is 'don't mess with the governor.' Your feelings have nothing to do with it. Be cool. If you are hurt it is advisable to not make a big deal of that side of things. Absorb the pain of your child's rebellion. Try not to take it personally when your children are naughty. They are simply doing what children do. In as far you are hurt, let it go, remembering God's grace to you a sinner. If your child is mature enough to recognise and repent of the hurt they have done to you then of course you must grant forgiveness. But that does not mean you backtrack on the need for obedience. When they disobey a parent, the offence is chiefly against God and if it is appropriate you can encourage them to seek forgiveness from him.

### 3. Here we go again

Practice makes perfect. This is the long haul. Ask God for patience to see this training through. There will be days in the twos and threes when you feel you are making the same point over and over again. And sometimes by bedtime you are wrung out. But rejoice in the fact that your child does not bear grudges and that she is going to bed very secure because she is in no doubt about who is in charge. And every morning is new—a brand new page with no blots on it. While you might carry a heavy heart overnight, your little daughter rises with bright eyes and a smile. It is a new opportunity to learn. Match her smile with your own. She is work in progress.

### Some practical inferences and applications

1. Since your word in your home is a small reflection of God's

word to us, you need to ensure consistency. Not only must you follow through on instructions and see that they are obeyed, you also must be meticulous about keeping your promises, even when this is inconvenient.

2. The framework of obedience is the framework not a straightjacket. Are you within that framework giving plenty of space and freedom? Consider God's word to Adam in the garden, 'You are free to eat from any tree in the garden; but you must not eat ...' In other words don't be on their case all the time about everything. When do your children get to enjoy some liberty?

## For further reading

'Aren't they lovely when they're asleep' by Ann Benton (Christian Focus)

'Shepherding a child's heart' by Tedd Tripp (Shepherd Press)

# Chapter 6

# The rod of correction

## Is the naughty step all we need?

*A 4 year old child was explaining what happened at home when he was naughty. He said, 'My Mummy sends me to my bedroom.' He paused and then smiled, and added, 'I like it there.'*

The law (in England and Wales) recognises that parents have responsibilities, for example, to feed, clothe and house their children. Parents who fail in those areas are liable to prosecution for neglect. Parents are also legally responsible to ensure that if they have children of statutory school age their children receive an education suitable to their needs. In order to carry out those responsibilities the law also recognises that parents have power to control and direct their children and that this is a unique and non-reciprocal role.

For centuries parents have understood that in order to control and direct their children they might be called upon to use physical means as a sanction against their children. In 1860 the defence of 'reasonable chastisement' was established in law as a defence against prosecution for assault and battery, if a parent was brought to trial. In 2004 the law changed to restrict the circumstances in which the 'reasonable chastisement' defence can be used. It can only be used now in relation to a charge of common assault, but not in relation to a charge of assault causing actual, or grievous, bodily harm. (Section 58, Children Act 2004)

What does that mean, in common speak? It means that if a parent uses physical means to punish a child, the physical damage done to the child via that punishment must be no more than superficial and temporary e.g. a slight reddening of the skin, which quickly fades. Grazes, bruises and abrasions would constitute actual bodily harm and there is no reasonable chastisement defence there. This does not make minor smacking legal. Assault remains a criminal offence. It merely means that a parent who is prosecuted for common assault can raise the defence of reasonable chastisement. Such cases rarely come to court because of the availability of that defence and because it would not normally be considered to be in the public interest. Whether this shift in the law has protected any child is dubious. And of course the law may change again.

In 2004 a lot of journalistic ink was employed in debating this issue. 'These people telling me how to chastise my child need a slap,' was the headline of one pro-smacking feature writer.

But more overall media attention was given to the lobby groups who wanted, but did not get, a complete ban on smacking. They made noise about the horrors of violence inflicted on children and the irreparable damage that corporal punishment can do. Nobody would have disagreed with them in relation to the tragic cases they named, in particular the brutal treatment and murder of Victoria Climbie. But as the chairman of the Kent Police Federation, writing in the Police Review wrote at the time, 'the systematic and vile abuse of Victoria Climbie was not done by people who failed to understand the boundaries of the 1860 defence of reasonable chastisement.' In other words the defence of reasonable chastisement has never been a child abusers' charter.

My experience in running parenting courses up and down the country is that this whole issue remains controversial. It is not uncommon for me to detect a sharp intake of breath when I mention smacking as one of the range of sanctions available to parents. Some parents actually think it has been outlawed. It is certainly true that many official bodies behave as if it has been.

## What does the Bible say?
Here is a sample of some sayings from the book of Proverbs on this subject:

> Whoever spares the rod hates his son,
> but he who loves him is diligent to discipline him.     Proverbs 13:24

> Whoever spares the rod hates his son,
> but he who loves him is diligent to discipline him.     Proverbs 22:15

> Do not withhold discipline from a child;
> if you strike him with a rod, he will not die.

If you strike him with the rod,
you will save his soul from Sheol.                    Proverbs 23:13–14

I am well aware that Proverbs is wisdom not precepts. It is a book saying how things tend to work in God's world. And what these proverbs seem to be saying is that the exercise of painful sanctions is a parental duty.

## Some Biblical principles of punishment

### 1. Punishment is necessary

When in 2004 I wrote to the MP for Guildford about the smacking issue, I was not surprised to discover that she, as a Liberal Democrat, supported an outright ban. She was, she wrote, in favour of parents using more positive means to manage the behaviour of their children. I did not enter into a correspondence with her to find out exactly what she meant. Did she mean bribe them? Or excuse them? Or merely jolly them along? Such alternatives to discipline were examined and found wanting in the last chapter. But if a parent thinks she can raise a child and always be positive, she is probably in for a shock.

Of course punishment is only one part of a discipline strategy which includes instruction, encouragement and correction. Verbal prohibitions and of course, reasoning, where the child is capable of it, are both in the mix at some stage. But at the end of the line in the face of defiance or rebellion towards a parent's stated and comprehended instruction or prohibition, sanctions, which are by definition negative, have to be brought in. Otherwise the parent's authority is toothless.

When the apostle Paul writes about the power of the state to wield the sword, he describes the one in authority as 'God's servant for your good'. (Romans 13:1–5) Similarly the authority God gives to parents is to include the power to punish the wrongdoer, for his or her good.

By wrongdoing I mean that a clearly defined line has been crossed. This is not hitting out in anger—anger has no place in punishment. It is not for some childish mistake. The Bible in Deuteronomy 19 distinguishes between the axe-swinger who inadvertently sends the loose head of the axe into an unfortunate neighbour and the man who kills with 'malice aforethought'. For the former there is clemency, for the latter there is the full weight of the law. Motive is hugely significant. Do not just judge by results. The most serious crime a child could commit in Old Testament Israel was to curse his father or mother. (Exodus 21:17) That shows how very important respect for parents is in God's book. A parent is right to disallow backchat and attitude. God does not like it.

There are various sanctions which are at a parent's disposal. Sometimes natural consequences of bad behaviour themselves teach a child a lesson; sometimes logical consequences suggest themselves, for example a child who behaves in an anti-social manner is removed temporarily from society i.e. sent to his bedroom. But sometimes a parent is dealing with what is effectively a challenge to parental authority and therefore action needs to be taken to undergird that authority and demonstrate to the child that such behaviour is wrong and has to stop.

Punishment is both necessary and right. Modern parents

believe in encouraging good behaviour,—it is generally what they do best even for behaviour which is morally dubious. Surely therefore it is logical also to make clear your disapproval of bad behaviour. If a child is responsible for good behaviour and therefore meriting praise, surely he is also responsible for bad behaviour and therefore meriting censure.

> If the righteous is repaid on earth,
> how much more the wicked and the sinner!          Proverbs 11:31

## 2. Punishment is the act of a loving parent

The anti-smacking lobby would like to criminalise parents who physically punish their children labelling them monsters or abusers. The Bible however says that it is the act of a loving parent to punish a naughty child. It assumes that its readers would understand that their parents punished them when they were children for their own good; this is a picture of what God does with us when he introduces hardship into our lives. God is merely treating us as any loving father would. So runs the argument of Hebrews 12:7-11.

'It is for discipline that you have to endure. God is treating you as sons. For what son is there whom his father does not discipline? If you are left without discipline, in which all have participated, then you are illegitimate children and not sons. Besides this, we have had earthly fathers who disciplined us and we respected them. Shall we not much more be subject to the Father of spirits and live? For they disciplined us for a short time as it seemed best to them, but he disciplines us for our good, that we may share his holiness. For the moment all discipline seems painful rather than pleasant, but later

it yields the peaceful fruit of righteousness to those who have been
trained by it.' Hebrews 12:7–11

The outcome of such discipline and punishment at the hands of
God is that we become better people. 'Before I was afflicted I went
astray, but now I keep your word,' records the psalmist in Psalm
119:67. This is the motivation of any loving parent who punishes a
child.

Proverbs 13:24, quoted above, goes as far as saying that a failure
in this area is indicative of hatred rather than love. A parent who
flunks the necessary reasonable punishment of his offspring is
doing them no favours. A consideration of the parenting style
of Eli as told in 1 Samuel 2 and 3 shows that failure to correct
transgressing children brought destruction to his whole house. Eli
rebuked his sons but when they failed to listen it seems he left it at
that. God held Eli accountable for that failure.

The implication of Proverbs 23:13–14 is that there is also
spiritual gain to be had for the offspring of parents who are
unflinching with 'the rod'. In contrast to those who say that
irreparable harm is done to children who are smacked, the Bible
at this point is saying that long-term irreparable harm may be
done to those who are not. Children recover very quickly from
a smacked bottom. Hugs and smiles are important at that point.
But children may be damaged eternally by being allowed to
go through life without recognising legitimate authority. Not
to mention the psychological damage in their lifetime which
is an outcome of some of smacking's alternatives: verbal
abuse, shouting, screaming, shutting away and other forms of
humiliation and rejection.

The idea of the violence of smacking also deserves a challenge. Is a surgeon violent when he takes a very sharp knife and cuts a child's flesh? We would not call it so for we would accept that the unpleasant and intrusive aspects of surgery are all towards a good and therapeutic end. So it is with the punishment of a child. You can describe it as violent but it might also be described as therapeutic. Certainly my husband and I discovered our children were a lot pleasanter for it.

## 3. Punishment has to be unpleasant

This is the point that well-meaning politicians have sometimes failed to recognise. They stand up in the House of Commons and say 'Smacking is not very nice.' Of course it is not. What punishment would work if it were nice? I refer you to the admission of the 4 year old related at the start of this chapter. Admittedly the child might be talking down the punishment as an act of bravado, but his admission points up the issue that if a child is unfazed by a punishment, that punishment is unlikely to be effective in changing his behaviour.

The message that a punishment has to give is the very strong disapproval of a parent and the determination on the part of the parent that the punishment will be unpleasant enough to make the child think twice about repeating the offence. The basic offence in question will always be related to a challenge to authority. In other words the child has been instructed and warned but has decided to ignore both instruction and warning.

## Now what next?

The naughty step is the modern equivalent of what used to happen in schools when a child was sent to stand in the corner.

I have known children who feel the weight of the parent's displeasure at being made to go and sit at the bottom of the stairs. After a time they are restored to the bosom of the family having expressed due repentance. But I have also known children who rather enjoy the view from there. I have seen siblings who cheerfully and voluntarily go and join the naughty one on the step and have a fine chat. And most peculiar of all was the mother who in all seriousness told me that she always used the naughty step but that she had to hold the child on it.

Some parents find that withdrawal of privileges or toys is a very effective punishment because their children hate that so much. Others have said that they find that such measures can go on rather a long time and frankly are quite difficult to remember to police.

Smacking is an immediate, non-verbal response to defiance. I cannot state often enough that it is never about venting rage; in fact I say to parents, 'If you are angry, put your hands behind your back.' It should not be brutal and over the top and it will not be if the parent is not angry. But it sends a clear message; the issue is dealt with and the relationship is restored on the right footing— one that says that the parent is in charge and mutiny will not be tolerated.

It really is up to the parent to decide which sanction works. I would defend the right of a parent to not smack his child as much as I would the right of a parent to smack. The key is: know your child. A parent knows her child better than anyone and I invite parents to be unafraid to use a sanction which has the desired effect. Some children are brought to repentance by a parent's frown; most are not. Of our own four children some were rarely smacked, others had to learn the lesson again and again. Smacking was generally a thing of the past by the time our children started primary school. After that they each knew that they had to do as we said, and a firm reminder was enough. This also is something I have often heard from the lips of parents who admit to having smacked their children. They talk about it as something which made other lesser sanctions more effective and therefore was rarely done.

## Questions parents ask

### 1. Is the rod a metaphor?

Most Christian parents have no problem with the idea of punishment and understand that it has to hurt. But instinctively they are unwilling to get physical and they look on the rod idea from Proverbs as metaphorical. After all, they challenge me, did you actually use a rod? My answer is that I did not use any implement (although I know people who did), but just my bare hand. So yes in one sense I think that the rod is a metaphor for punishment of a child by his parent. But it surely has to be a metaphor which includes the idea of the physical or the Bible is leading us truly in a wrong direction.

We are all products of our upbringing and many contemporary people are squeamish and against any kind of physical confrontation even in a just cause. But the Bible says:

'Blows that wound cleanse away evil;
strokes make clean the innermost parts.'         Proverbs 20:30

Surely that means that sometimes it takes a painful experience to make us change our ways. If the naughty step is painful, then send them there, but do not too quickly rule out the expedient which has been proved to be a simple and useful corrective by generations of quite wise, loving and rational parents before you.

## 2. Are smacked children more aggressive?

The reason many parents do not smack their children is that they think that their children will learn merely that hitting people is OK. In other words to smack is to set a bad example. 'Here am I,' says a mother, 'telling my child that he must not hit others, and then I go and hit him.'

The answer to that is that there is a massive difference between a child hitting another child and a parent administering a smack to reinforce a declared prohibition.

- A child hitting another is hitting in anger and frustration; whereas a parental smack is calm and controlled and related to training.

- A child's relationship with another child is not one of authority; whereas a parental smack is authoritative—the parent is the only one allowed to do this.

- A child has no business disciplining another child; but it is the act of a loving parent to discipline.

There is no actual evidence that smacked children are more aggressive. Of course such evidence would be almost impossible to gather because of the wide range of other factors in a child's life. But if there is any evidence it would be that smacked children are rather less likely to be aggressive with others. Think about the baby boomer generation born in the decade or so after WWII. Nearly every child in that generation met the rod, i.e. physical correction, perhaps quite frequently and often in anger. But aggression from children in primary schools was pretty rare. Certainly aggression towards adults was almost unknown. But a poll of primary school teachers conducted by the Association of Teachers and Lecturers in 2009 found that almost two thirds had witnessed physical aggression from their pupils. Any reception class teacher will tell you how commonplace is aggressive behaviour. And this is from a generation whose parents are less likely to have used corporal punishment than any previous generation.

Of course there are some children for whom smacking would never be appropriate, for example children who have been adopted from an abusive background. And of course, the rod does not stand alone in a parent's discipline strategy; there is plenty of room for patient correction and instruction. In particular, the rod, whatever you take that to mean, will only be effective in the context of a warm relationship. For decades research into children behaviour has found that firmness on a foundation of real affection is a winning combination in producing happy, secure and well-behaved children. One of the latest of such studies, published in 2013 in the journal Parenting: Science and Practice found the painful effects of discipline, including smacking, were offset by the child's feeling of being loved.

### 3. If smacking is not about anger, what is it for?

It is easy to lose sight of what all this is about. It is about training children in obedience; it is about teaching them to respect authority; it is about helping them to know their place in the universe; it is for their good, for a 'peaceful fruit of righteousness' (Hebrews 12:11). You will know when it is working: the sign will be that you raise a child who is respectful, who can admit a fault and learn from it. This is quite a deep work and may take years of practice. But there are dozens of Proverbs which say that this is a most encouraging sign for a parent.

> 'A fool despises his father's instruction,
> but whoever heeds reproof is prudent.'          Proverbs 15:5

> 'The ear that listens to life-giving reproof
> will dwell among the wise.'          Proverbs 15:31

## Some practical inferences and applications

1. Consider your response to your child's misbehaviour. Are you inclined to explode when your children irritate you? Think about ways to be a thermostat, not a thermometer, and be proactive in a situation where you might be likely to lose it if the temperature continues to rise. Perhaps you could step in earlier to divert, distract or separate, rather than explode when something is the last straw.

2. How does your child respond to correction? Is your child of an age to respond to a chat about his duty to his parents, who must also give an account to God about their training of him? The missionary Amy Carmichael, as a child, was taught to thank her father after he smacked her. This might seem a bit over the top but it does recognise the fact that discipline rightly administered really is doing our children a favour.

# Chapter 7

# Manly boys and feminine girls

## Gender distinctives without stereotyping

*The makers of Kinder Surprise have been criticised for reinforcing gender stereotypes, after launching a limited edition range of pink and blue eggs. Those in pink packaging will contain dolls; the blue ones toy cars. A spokesman from Ferrero denied that its product was 'gender specific,' insisting that the packaging would merely help parents choose the right product for their child.*

Reported in The Week 10th August 2013

P eople are very touchy about gender these days. Or to be very specific members of one gender are very touchy. I can't recall ever hearing a member of the male sex complaining about blue clothing or about being denied the opportunity to play with dolls.

In contemporary media generally there is a dominant anti-marriage, anti-masculine ideology. In advertising the women are the smart sassy ones and the men are the idiots. In the popular TV detective series, Scott and Bailey, the two female detectives and their female boss are surrounded by male colleagues who inevitably turn out to be either clots or cheats. The children's film animation, Brave, had a feisty young female heroine (nothing wrong with that) whose happy ending was to avoid marriage and to outsmart and outperform the completely clueless men in her entourage, including her father who was a drunken thug.

While the spoken mantra is that gender is irrelevant and that male/female is a social construct which should bring with it no preconceptions, the undercurrent is that men generally have the monopoly on stupidity and it is only the 'glass ceiling' and the historical oppression of women by men which is preventing the rise and rise of women who would undoubtedly make the world a better place.

Let us remind ourselves of what the Bible teaches about gender:

## 1. God made male and female

'So God created man in his own image,
in the image of God he created him;
male and female he created them.'                    Genesis 1:27

'He (Jesus) answered, "Have you not read that he who created them from the beginning made them male and female"'

Matthew 19:4

There always have been two genders, by design. God could have created a unisex mankind, but he did not. The Genesis account is both history and symbolism. We live in a designed universe, not a random one. The words of Jesus underscore the Creator's declared intention: to make humankind in two distinct genders. The apostle Paul in several places draws on the details of Genesis 1–3 to unpack God's great purposes in the universe. So it is no overstatement to say that a foundational aspect of any person's identity is gender.

## 2. Male and female are equal in value

Genesis 1:27 tells us that both men and women equally bear the image of God. They were equally given what is called the creation mandate of Genesis 1:28, to rule over the earth. Genesis 3 tells us that both were guilty in listening to the serpent rather than trusting God. Both were held accountable and were punished; their progeny was forever after flawed, equally. And when God sent the Saviour he redeemed men and women, equally.

Writing to the Galatian church (Galatians 3:28) Paul reminds believers that whatever their gender or racial or ethnic background, they all entered God's family by the same door: the door of faith in Christ. The clothing of Christ gives no higher status to one kind over another. God has paid the same price for each, the precious blood of Christ. They are equally wanted and loved by God.

## 3. Men and women are different by design

It is quite possible for items which are equal in value to be entirely different. Difference in itself does not imply superiority or inferiority. God designed men and women to be different, although they have much in common. They were made from different materials and were each given a particular focus (Genesis 2:7, 22, 15, 18). Man was made from the ground and work was to be his particular focus; woman was made from man and was given a relational focus—to be a helper.

You do not have to have any grounding in anatomy to observe that men and women have quite incontrovertible biological differences, especially, but not exclusively, in reproductive function. One initiates life in procreation; the other carries and nurtures the new life. A man's strongest muscles are in his upper body; a woman's are in her uterus. But there are physiological and psychological differences too. The website 'Masters of Healthcare' lists ten. Here is a sample:

- Brain size—the male brain is typically 10% larger

- Brain hemispheres—men are sharply left-brain dominant; women tend to use right and left brain simultaneously

- Mathematical skills—the part of the brain which controls numerical brain function is larger in males than in females

- Language—the brain areas that deal with language and communication are larger in females

- Emotions—women tend to have a larger deep limbic system than men: this is the part that controls emotions

- Spatial awareness—in the female brain the parietal region is thicker, which limits spatial ability in women.

Now of course we all remember the girl at school who always beat the boys in maths tests, and the female East German shot-putter who could have thrown Brad Pitt into next week. We recognise that there is a spectrum of individual differences in each gender; even so, the differences are generally beyond dispute.

## Biblical manhood and womanhood

John Piper has written extensively and helpfully on this subject, underlining the fact that the Bible's teaching on the differing roles men and women have in relation to each other is based not on temporary cultural norms but on permanent facts of creation. (1 Corinthians 11:3–16; Ephesians 5:21–33; 1 Timothy 2:11–14). He has also attempted a definition of Biblical manhood and womanhood, admitting that this is a very risky business and adding that these definitions are not exhaustive. But I quote them here because I cannot improve on them.

'At the heart of mature masculinity is a sense of benevolent responsibility to lead, provide for and protect women in ways appropriate to a man's differing relationships.'

'At the heart of mature femininity is a freeing disposition to affirm, receive and nurture strength and leadership from worthy men in ways appropriate to a woman's differing relationships.'

Readers may want to quibble about some of the words or phrases in the above, or indeed about the whole thrust, but I would refer you to Piper's own unpacking of his statements in the book named at the end of this chapter. I use those definitions as a place to start as we return to our theme which is the raising of children.

## Gender implications and distinctions

Imagine, or recall, first hearing about the gender of your newborn baby, whether that is in the clean, calm clinicity of the scan experience, or in the heat of postpartum sweat, exhaustion and euphoria. What do you do with that information? What are its implications? Where does it take you in imagination and purpose? Perhaps your first thought is about the colour you will paint the nursery or about getting your beloved train set/ dolls house down from the loft. At this point we need to separate out the strands of gender differences, distinguishing between the absolute and the arbitrary, the benign and the pernicious.

### • Absolute distinctions

These are the differences mentioned above, to do with reproductive capability, brain function, relative strength and aptitudes. According to the Bible, a boy will grow up to marry a girl, if he marries; a girl will grow up to marry a boy, if she marries. She has a helper, people-centred, emotionally intuitive design; he has a leader, risk-taker, protective design.

### • Arbitrary distinctions

These are the cultural but benign distinctions, which work in terms of identification and social acceptability, like hair-length, clothing and which public toilet you go into. You can send your little boy to school in a skirt, to make a point, but you probably won't, unless you live in Scotland and the skirt is a kilt, because it would do him no favours. But these things are conventions and have no serious implications, (except for the boy who turns up at school in a skirt).

## • Pernicious stereotypes

Macho dominant aggression in boys is a cultural stereotype which is neither Biblical nor helpful. Equally malignant is the total focus on external appearance put on girls. There is no reason why a girl cannot play with an Action Man—though she will probably marry him to one of her dolls—or why a boy shouldn't enjoy baking. I leave the reader to think of more examples of cultural distinctions which are unnecessary or even damaging.

## • The feminist response

Since the beginning of the move, fifty years ago, to deconstruct the sexual difference, culture has been widely blamed wherever different outcomes for men and women are observed. Many attempts have been made to remove not merely the unhelpful distinctions but the benign ones and the absolute ones. 'Sexist' material, like Enid Blyton, has found itself banned from some libraries; firemen are fire-fighters; a chairman is a chairperson or, even worse, a chair; history is her story. We are supposed to believe that men and women are identical in attitudes and abilities and we are certainly not allowed to imply anywhere that heterosexual is the norm.

The alarming result has been that while God's design is defaced, pernicious gender differences are on the rise.

## The issue for boys: the feminisation/cissification of culture

The trouble with attacking the masculine absolutes is that it leaves a bit of a vacuum. The ideal now is the 'new man' who displays feminine characteristics: he is nurturant and supportive. There is no place for provider or protector: that would be interpreted as an insult to women, implying an incompleteness about her.

In the field of education, there has been concern about the under-achievement of boys. But teaching and assessment methods have largely ousted the active and competitive, which appeals to the risk-taking side of boys, and favoured the beautifully coloured-in coursework and the sedentary learning, which appeals to girls.

Even dietary advice favours the nutritional needs of girls: red meat, out; salads, in. But then, 95% of nutritionists are female.

So what does a growing boy do in the face of the new man ideal and the general cissification of culture. Nothing can stop him liking competitive team sports, war games and stories, so he is liable to take off in the direction of a laddish, loutish sub-culture. The nineties sitcom Men behaving badly was about two immature young men, characterised by drunkenness, vulgarity and a total disrespect for women. The characters were created as a joke. Much to the surprise of the actors involved they became heroes and role models for a generation of growing boys. They were a refuge for men who were uncomfortable with the new man.

Unless, that is, they will look in the Bible where we see man as God created him. Adam was created to be a king to provide, a warrior to protect, a mentor to instruct and a friend to connect.

That is the ideal we must keep in mind if we are in the business of raising boys in a feminised culture.

## The issue for girls: the sexualisation of culture and the demise of modesty

Alongside the feminisation of culture has been the sexualisation of culture. There are now no no-go areas for boys or for girls. Girls in particular are being taught that they must avoid any kind of passivity; instead they are encouraged to be brazen. They must be thrusting, pushing their way to the forefront. To show modesty or embarrassment is scorned as an unhealthy hang-up.

Christianity raised the status of women to where they had a right to the protection of men. It is well documented that a young woman travelling alone in Europe or North America in the early twentieth century was far safer than she would be now. No one would harm her, because she was a woman. Her modesty, alongside male chivalry, was itself a protection. Men would treat her as they would treat their sisters or mothers. In the sinking of the Titanic, the 'woman and children first' concept was unquestioned in the face of danger.

Jessica Rey can be found on Youtube lecturing on the evolution of swimwear. The bikini was invented in 1946 and named after the nuclear testing site Bikini Atoll, because of the explosive effect it was designed to have on men. She quotes research conducted by Professor Susan Fiske (cited CNN April 2009) at Princeton University which monitored the brain activity of men looking at girls in bikinis. Professor Fiske found that regions of the brain connected with tools were activated while the empathetic side was totally shut down. This was not the case when the same male students looked at pictures of women who were modestly attired. The conclusions were that immodest clothing reduced the possibility of a woman being seen as a person and increased the perception by a man of her as an object to be used.

Not that radical feminism has ever been that keen on bikinis, but is has encouraged girls to have a no holds barred approach to life. Romantic notions are discouraged. Sex is just an animal function, promoted to be initiated and enjoyed by women as much as men. Virginity is for prudes.

Meanwhile little girls are encouraged to dress as women. There are make-up parties for 6-year olds. In more and more of what they do, children are being enticed into the world of adult sexuality. Parents will march to rid their streets of paedophiles but will buy their little girls crop tops and allow them to watch children's TV with its obsession with pop/celebrity culture and the accompanying overt sexual display. Modesty is a lost concept.

Of course the feminists never wanted that to happen, but as has happened with masculinity, there is a vacuum in the role model department. The average girl does not want to be in competition with men. She has other ambitions although she dare not articulate them. So she takes refuge in the unhelpful stereotype— the babe—hung up with clothes, body shape and appearance. The Schools Health Education Unit found in 2006 that 60% of girls between the age of 12 and 15 wanted to lose weight while only 15% needed to. There is a near obsession with skeletal body shapes in the whole media and fashion industry which is where twenty-first century teenagers are inclined to look for role models.

The Bible shows us true womanhood whose beauty emanates from the inside. The advice to a young man looking for a wife is:

'Charm is deceitful, and beauty is vain,
but a woman who fears the Lord is to be praised.'          Proverbs 31:30

She is not a helpless female; she is a helper, not competing but completing. Parents have a strategic role in raising manly men and feminine girls. The rest of this chapter will explore how we might do that.

## Raising manly boys and feminine girls

### Children first

Although I have spent much of this chapter talking about the differences between men and women—because in the present cultural tide those are the things which are being crucially eroded—when a baby is born, he or she is first of all a child. God designed the reproductive machinery to kick in ten or more years down the road and so in that sense your baby is just a baby; your child is just a child. The differences, both psychological and physical, will emerge on their own over time. So the first thing is: let them be children and do not allow sex to rear its head before it needs to. Boys and girls can and should be encouraged to play together and given opportunity to engage in all kinds of activities. There is absolutely no need for stereotyping.

### The emergent personality

But as children grow and develop or reveal their tastes, talents and aptitudes, it is very common for gender to reveal itself along predictable lines. So here is a boy who brings his plastic dinosaur down to the breakfast table. The dinosaur is roaring and ready to fight. The boy's sister takes up the dinosaur, cuddles it and attempts to feed it Weetabix.

When my grandchildren arrive to visit our house they head for the toys, abandoned a generation ago by their parents, aunt and uncles. Nobody, least of all me, directs them, but strange to relate, the girls make a bee-line for the dolls house, the boy for the soldiers and cars.

There are exceptions of course and this should not perturb us. Gender sometimes emerges more slowly and there is a spectrum of gender-linked attributes which means that it is OK for a girl not to like playing with dolls or for a boy not to like competitive sports. Every child is God's unique creation.

## How children learn

But from the earliest possible age children are learning: they are receiving and interpreting messages. If we think about the mechanisms involved we may see a way forward. But before we even get to mechanisms, the first crucial fact about learning is that children learn from people and the most significant people in their lives are their parents.

Studies of children whose fathers are absent from home show a negative effect on sex-role development, especially on boys, but to some extent on girls. So the first thing a child needs in order to develop a healthy gender identity is the presence of two parents. Where this is impossible, other trustworthy adults may supply what is lacking.

Not only must the parents be present but the relationship needs to be warm. The degree of a father's warm involvement with his son has been found to be more important in healthy gender identity than explicit encouragement towards masculine behaviour. This is true for girls and their mothers too.

## Language

Language forms the hooks by which we organise our thoughts. So from infancy children's minds are being moulded by the words we use. The word shapes the concept, the concept shapes the idea, the idea will shape the opinion and the opinion will shape behaviour. But it starts with words. So use words which raise awareness of sexual identity. Keep alive in the language the notion of husband, wife, mother, father and all the other family nouns which are gender-specific. The old card game *Happy Families* is useful too. Get hold a pack before they are outlawed or morphed into something dysfunctional.

## Imitation

We all know how babies at a certain stage love to mirror activities. That is how you get a baby to blow a raspberry and then, later, wish you hadn't. Nearly everything an infant learns to do is by imitation. That means be aware of the kind of man and woman you are. If you as a mother are demonstrating Biblical femininity in demeanour and attitude, your daughters will want to grow up to be nurturant, completing and helping. Boys need to see their fathers providing, protecting, leading and connecting. They need to see an Ephesians 5 marriage.

A church family is also a place to find other role models, where a range of personalities express their manhood and womanhood, each in their unique way.

## Affirmation and censure

As children grow and seek a parent's approval, a parent has opportunity to shape behaviour and attitudes in the right direction. So some behaviour will meet warm encouragement while other behaviour will meet very clear disapproval. This can as appropriate be explicitly used to reinforce the correct role-modelling.

Beware of using praise, unwittingly to reinforce unhelpful stereotypes. So don't overdo the praise of little girls, lovely as they are, on how they look or on what they are wearing. That does not mean you have to pay no attention to appearance in girls or indeed boys. But you will not want to encourage preening so don't have too many mirrors about the place. It is wonderful to be beautiful : we worship a God who made a beautiful world for his glory. Your daughter may be decorative but don't let her be purely decorative. Praise attitude more than appearance. And avoid the treadmill of allowing her to dress for effect, wanting to inspire either envy or lust. In other words being beautiful is better than being attractive and in humans true beauty starts on the inside. You want your child to enjoy her childhood without being self-conscious. Self-forgetfulness is more fun and more fitting. Clothes need to be functional and freeing. I recall with sadness the little girl who always arrived at our children's club at church dressed in clothing reminiscent of night-life of Soho. Such attire, in particular the footwear, always impeded her participation in the games.

Sometimes a similar effect can be seen on boys who have been encouraged consciously or unconsciously by their elders in a macho direction which has nothing to do with Biblical manliness. Masculine strength is designed not for showing off or oppressing others but for serving and protecting. Let them use their superior strength to help. That is the kind of manliness to praise and encourage in your little boy.

## Experience and experimentation

More than by being told, children learn by doing. That is why it is important that they experience appropriate relationships with the adult men and women in their lives. But also they can learn gender identity by practice. They can practise leading, serving and helping. And they can try on roles through imaginative play. Through stories and films they can identify with heroes and heroines and you can talk through these and appreciate whatever is pure, lovely and commendable (Philippians 4:8).

## Interaction and instruction

Much interaction with small children is in play. This is where they try ideas out and toss them around. As they grow older, casual conversation where together you observe the world around you is also a crucial way of learning. Of course, children do not learn simply by being told, but parents should not shy away from being quite clear about what the Bible teaches about gender, sex and marriage. Be explicit about who is head of the home and about the fact that the head of the home will answer to God for his leadership of the family. Ask them whether they can spot the lie or the unhelpful stereotypes in certain advertisements or other media.

## Some practical inferences and applications

1. Think about your children's clothing. One of the uses of clothing is to make gender unambiguous. This is expressed along cultural lines but remains both useful and right. Deuteronomy 22:5 tells us that God detests cross-dressing. But alongside putting your boys and girls in gender-appropriate clothing, consider the issue of modesty. Look inside your daughter's wardrobe. Is her natural sense of modesty being eroded by promiscuous dress? It can be a challenge, not least with the daughter in question, but channel her in the direction of pretty but modest. Teach her that modest does not mean frumpy and dumpy.

2. It is, sadly, more important than ever to be selective about reading and watching material. Some stories are written with the explicit aim of undermining absolute gender distinctions. Others reinforce unhelpful stereotypes: shallow princesses, rough and rude boys. You may have to go back to some classics for the best in children's stories: Swallows and Amazons, Anne of Green Gables, Narnia. In these stories the girls are not wimps but they are feminine and the boys are brave and moral. Don't despise such books because they come from another century. They still entertain. *The Dangerous Book for Boys* by Conn and Hal Iggulden has been a surprise bestseller filling a gap in a feminised market. They conjure up a childhood marked by adventure and innocence. A more recent publication is 'Amazing tales for making men out of boys' by Neil Oliver. And there are others of that kind. The Victorian writer Anthony Trollope said that he wrote his stories to teach the men to be honest and the girls that modesty is a charm well worth preserving. I like him for it.

## For further reading:

'Recovering Biblical Manhood and Womanhood' edited by John
   Piper and Wayne Grudem (Crossway Books)

'Gender Questions' by John Benton (Evangelical Press)

'A Return to Modesty' by Wendy Shalit (Free Press)

'The Miseducation of Women' by James Tooley (Continuum)

'Why Men don't Iron' by Anne and Bill Moir (Harper/Collins)

'God's design for women' by Sharon James (EP)

# Chapter 8

# Sex and the Christian family

## Countering the secular lies about love, sex and marriage

*5 year old James had just had his best friend Harry to play. As his mother, Kate, closed the door having waved off Harry and his dad, she turned to James to ask him if he had had a good time. 'Oh yes,' said James, 'I love Harry. I am going to marry him when I grow up.' Kate smiled and explained to James that he was a little boy and that little boys grew up to be men and that men marry women. 'Like Daddy and me,' she said. 'Daddy is a man and I'm a woman.'*

*James accepted this explanation but a few days later he came out of*

*school and told Kate, 'I told Harry what you said but Harry said his*
*Mummy says that boys can marry boys.'*

I t's official. It is now legally possible in England and Wales for
boys to marry boys and girls to marry girls. In a primetime
quiz show a male contestant being interviewed about his life
refers to the fact that he lives with his husband, Jim. Nobody
bats an eyelid. On the contrary, there are many who genuinely
celebrate this shift in attitude as a breakthrough as wonderful as
the abolition of slavery.

In some ways it is ironic that this is happening at a time when
marriage itself as an institution is declining in popularity. Married
people are now in a minority in England and Wales, having fallen
from 51% of the population in 2001 to 47% in 2011. There is also
evidence that marriage is increasingly the province of the graduate
class; for financial and other reasons the labouring classes are
much less likely to commit. And although the divorce rate is lower
than it was, no doubt linked to the decline in marriage, it is still
high. Based on marriage statistics from 2010, it is estimated that
42% marriages in the UK will end in divorce.

Meanwhile, according to the Family Planning Association the
UK has the highest teenage birth and abortion rates in Western
Europe. Television and films routinely portray and normalise sex
before and outside of marriage.

The incidence of sexually transmitted diseases continues to rise,
particularly amongst young people. Two thirds of new clinical
diagnoses in 2009 among women were in the 15–24 age bracket

and over half of new diagnoses among men. Men who have sex with men are especially at risk.

These facts on their own are enough to make Christian parents fear the onset of puberty in their children. This is not just against the tide: it is in the face of a howling gale. But the smiling liberal political and media elite, with their terribly nice line about there being 'many different ways of doing family' refuses to recognise what is in front of them and labels faithful Christian believers as the nasty party.

But God, our Creator and loving heavenly Father, has decreed the way to do family. Other ways may seem very accepting and affirming but they are a very poor choice for personal health and happiness and the common good. Dozens of studies over a considerable time show that the major factor in the development of happy, well-adjusted young people who keep off drugs, out of prison and do well at school is the presence of a mother and father who are married.

But let us leave statistics behind and turn to the Bible.

## Foundational Issues

### 1. Heterosexual marriage is God's idea

Marriage is defined in the Bible as a lifelong union between one man and one woman.

Jesus quotes Genesis 2:24 when he says:

He answered, 'Have you not read that he who created them from the beginning made them male and female, and said, "Therefore a man shall leave his father and his mother and hold fast to his wife, and the two shall become one flesh'"          Matthew 19:4–5

The word translated 'wife' is the word for woman. It is unequivocally female.

Marriage signifies the ending of one thing and the starting of something new, significant and lasting. A person leaves the parental home and in covenant with a partner inaugurates a new family, which is to be a building block of society and a proper context for the raising of the children, who are a fruit of that sexual union.

Marriage in the Bible has significance beyond human health and happiness, although it certainly promotes those. Marriage is designed to mirror a bigger union—that of Christ and the church. In Ephesians 5:31 Paul quotes Genesis 2:24 and then adds:

'This mystery is profound, and I am saying that it refers to Christ and the church.'          Ephesians 5:32

In the instruction about how marriage is to operate on earth Paul tells husbands that Christ is the model head. As Christ loves the church, a man must love his wife. And wives are to submit to their husbands as the church submits to Christ, gladly and respectfully. That is the blueprint for marriage and a marriage after this pattern is supposed to be a picture to a watching world of the greater mystery—Jesus and his amazing relationship with his bride, the church.

So there is another reason why no human government has the right to muck about with marriage. It is a huge divine concept, a creation ordinance.

Some people want to say that surely a loving and committed relationship between two people of the same gender is just as valid a picture. It is not. Not only would you fail to find anywhere in Scripture God's endorsement of such an idea (quite the reverse, actually, e.g. Leviticus 18:22) the whole point is that in a marriage you have the coming together of two people who are fundamentally different. They are both the same in that they each bear the image of God but they are also very distinct by virtue of their genders.

The God of the Bible is a Trinitarian God: one God, three persons, Father, Son and Holy Spirit. This trinity is the ultimate society, where you have a union of three who are the same but different. Heterosexual marriage mirrors that unity in diversity. Homosexual 'marriage' never could.

## 2. Humankind is made for relationship

God has made us for relationship. First of all we are made for relationship with him. Before their disobedience made a horrible divide, Adam and Eve walked with God in the bliss of Eden. In a fallen world our hearts still ask for God. Foolish and wayward as we are we all have a tendency to make God-substitutes.

God made us also to relate to each other and his word gives us guidelines and boundaries on how to pursue relationships of different kinds. The ten commandments (Exodus 20:1–17) remind us that our relationship with God is to be exclusive, involving a proper respect for his name and the regular setting aside of time for him. In our relationships with people we are to respect their lives, their property and their reputations. Our parents are to be honoured—that is a very special relationship. Marriage is also a protected relationship—faithfulness is crucial, again characterised by an exclusiveness which mirrors God's relationship with his people. So sex is just for marriage, a physical expression of the intimacy of that very special relationship between a husband and wife.

## Issues for parents to raise

Since marriage is such a central image in the Bible from Genesis to Revelation, Christian parents have every possible inducement to teach their children carefully about marriage. This is all the more important in an age when homosexuality is considered a positive lifestyle choice, virginity is a joke and cohabitation is the norm even where it eventually leads to marriage.

Christians have traditionally been very reluctant to talk to their children about sex. This is not Biblical. In the book of Proverbs a father talks to his probably adolescent son at length on the subject, recognising that the onset of puberty makes it a dominant part of a teenager's thought-life. The Song of Solomon, while being a beautiful picture of the love relationship between a believer and Christ, is still a graphic description of courtship and the sexual side of marriage.

It is also unhelpful to be silent when we live in such a sexed-up world. Do we want our children to learn about sex from TV or the internet or their friends or from sex education lessons at school? Get in first, and get in with a positive message.

## 1. Marriage is good

Instead of just tut-tutting about the lax morals of others, make sure your children understand that marriage is one of God's best ideas and a really worthy aim for their lives. Of course you will want to warn your children about the dangers of being sucked into sexual experimentation and of unhelpful early liaisons, but do so in a context of looking forward to future happiness. This is what the father does in Proverbs 5. Having spelled out the dangers of illicit sex, he waxes poetic as he anticipates the future lifelong married bliss of his son.

> 'a lovely deer, a graceful doe.
> Let her breasts fill you at all times with delight;
> be intoxicated always in her love.
> Why should you be intoxicated, my son, with a forbidden woman?'
>
> Proverbs 5:19–20

In other words, don't go for second best. The joys, including the physical joys, of marriage far exceed any guilty fumbling pleasures at the school disco.

My observation as a pastor's wife for over thirty years is that Christian parents are better at giving a positive message about marriage to their daughters then they are to their sons. Girls, being relational and tending towards the romantic, are more ready to receive such a message. Boys however, growing up in a culture which has embraced unadulterated narcissism, are all too inclined to throw out the baby with the bath water. They avoid both sex and marriage and find safety in numbers, hanging out with other boys in a perpetuated adolescence. Sometimes they fill the gap in their lives with computer games. A growing boy needs to understand that it is part of becoming a man to use your manhood for the service of others, and that to find a worthy girl to love and marry is a godly ambition for him, which will bring him immense delight.

'He who finds a wife finds a good thing and obtains favour from the Lord.'                                                  Proverbs 18:22

## 2. Sex is great

Christians have rather retreated on sex, acknowledging that it is God's idea but handing it over to the world to demoralise and demean it and turn it into little more than an animal function. But God intended it to be the supreme expression of tender, loving commitment between a man and woman in covenanted union, a source of consolation as well as procreation.

'Let marriage be held in honour among all, and let the marriage bed be undefiled, for God will judge the sexually immoral and adulterous.'                                                   Hebrews 13:4

Sometimes we have heard the thunder of the second half of that verse, and missed the sunshine of the first half. Marriage is good; there is nothing dodgy about sex in marriage—quite the opposite. Have we believed the world's lie that purity equals squeaky clean and is somewhat unpleasant? Purity is beautiful and it works well alongside joy. The sex scenes in the Song of Songs throb with passion and exuberant sensual delight. The sex in Christian marriages has every excuse to be nothing less. And the trust engendered by declared commitment and a shared history should only serve to enhance the experience.

Now, of course you will want to spare your children's blushes. Teenagers tend to gag at the thought of their parents having a sex life. But despite that, a Christian husband and wife should, within appropriate bounds, make no secret of the fact that they rather enjoy being alone together.

You would not want to jeopardise your daughter's future marriage by giving her too sanitised a view. Marriage, even Christian marriage, has its earthy side; it is not merely playing house. Let her understand that there is rather more involved. One of the things you do in marriage is gladly give your body to your marriage partner. (1 Corinthians 7:3–4)

## 3. Virginity is cool

The other side of that particular coin is the issue of waiting for marriage. Control of the sexual drive is something a teenager, sometimes taken by surprise by what his or her body gets up to, has to be taught and helped with in an age where apparently everyone else is 'doing it'.

Virginity up to the point of marriage is both godly and wise. You will sometimes hear the 'it's ok if you love each other' argument but the Bible is clear that the covenant (the binding promises made at the start of marriage) precedes sexual union and the New Testament word translated in the ESV 'sexual immorality' includes all sexual activity outside of marriage. (e.g. Colossians 3:5, Ephesians 5:3; 1 Corinthians 6:18).

Many young people engage in intercourse to raise their status with their friends or because they think it is expected. Afterwards they are filled with guilt and regrets that they gave something precious away so cheaply. And of course there is the risk of the misery of an unwanted pregnancy or sexually transmitted diseases. God's boundaries are a protection for young people from all of this. They spell liberty in the sense of freeing a young person to explore a range of friendships without making stupid mistakes which might ruin a life.

So when all the talk in sex education lessons will be about staying safe by going for screening and using a condom, the Christian parent will want to say that the way to stay safe is to stick to the firm policy of saying 'no' to all sexual pressure. Not just safe but pure and right. It makes sense.

## 4. Singleness is fine

While God has designed marriage as a normal part of being grown up and living as an adult, he has also made it clear that to stay single and, by implication, celibate is also a valid and good choice. Jesus of Nazareth never married and neither have many of his notable followers since. They stayed single and used their singleness to serve God without the burden of any dependants. Some people are cut out for the single life, long-term, and some are not, but of course everyone is single until they are married and there is no shame in it. As parents we need to encourage our children to embrace their singleness and use it well. It brings with it particular opportunities which married people do not have and they can make the most of those.

Peer group pressure which says you must be really seriously ugly or weird if you are not 'with' anyone must be resisted by encouraging our children to find their sense of self-worth in Christ and in his love.

## 5. The importance of friendship

Youth is a wonderful time for making lasting friends and parents will want to encourage their children in the art of friendship, which includes being loyal (Proverbs 17:17), a good listener (James 1:19), kind (Proverbs 11:16), forbearing (Proverbs 12:16) and avoiding gossip (Proverbs 17:9). While being generally friendly, they need to choose their friends carefully. (Proverbs 22:24) There is also a period in teenage life when, (particularly) girls can fall in and out with each other at the click of a text. That is why training in the Biblical social skills named above will help your children to steer a sane path and will protect them from a good deal of pain. It is helpful for them also to recognise that there are levels in friendship. Somewhere, sometime I read about them as the ABCD of friendship. Even Jesus Christ had levels of friendship: he had the multitude; he had the twelve; he had the three.

A. Acquaintance level: these are the many people whose names you know and maybe a few facts about them. To such people you are polite but you are not close in any sense. They walk in and out of your life.

B. Brotherly level: this will be a smaller number. You not only know these people but what they are about. You know something of their past and of their future plans and hopes, their likes and dislikes. You can have fun with such people, play with them, work alongside them. You can talk together about your opinions and interests. You can ask for help or be asked.

C. Commitment level: this is a relationship which through time has become much deeper. These are people with whom you have built up a shared history. It would include members of your family but also close friends. A Bible example would be David and Jonathan (1 Samuel 18:1–4). With these people you have shared interests, similar values, common goals and a mutual attraction. I need to stress in these sad days that it is quite possible to have such a friendship without a sexual component. Your relationship would be characterised by trust and by perseverance (Proverbs 18:24). You have seen them on their bad days and you still care about them. There would also be accountability in this relationship— you are able mutually to give and receive kindly words of correction. (Proverbs 27:6) If your child is a Christian, most of the people at this level should be Christians—friends from church or the Christian Union or from camp—and they are the kind you keep for life. Of course it is fine to have friends at this level who are not believers but be careful to never ever underestimate the gap between you. You are on different roads. (Matthew 7:13–14)

D. Devotion level: Out of those at the commitment level, one may emerge as particularly special to you—one of the opposite gender to whom you have a sexual attraction as well. This is the one you will want to pursue with a view to marriage—that life-long, home-making, family-raising commitment which is marriage. A Christian can only marry a Christian. That makes pragmatic sense; it is also Biblical truth. (1 Corinthians 7:39) Not to see this is blind ignorance, wishful thinking or wilful disobedience.

Some of the relationship muddle and mayhem teenagers get into derives from an inadequate understanding of friendship.

But even the most careful training in the art of friendship will not necessarily deliver a Christian parent from some thorny, even distasteful questions. So the final section of this chapter is about those.

## Issues parents would rather not face

### 1. Going out/dating

Young people grow up extremely quickly these days. You may do your best to hold this back but in the end you will be as successful King Canute was at holding back the waves. It does sometimes happen that a fifteen year old girl meets a boy in Bible Class who is the love of her life. I know happily married adults whose relationship began that young or younger. The besotted young couple want to date. What do you the parent do? First of all you thank God that your daughter is normal and that she has asked you about this. Keep the doors of communication open and keep calm. It is not for me to tell the readers of this book where to set the boundaries. You will know your children best and know what level of trust to offer. Many parents encourage their school-age children to wait rather than date. Others allow some limited and monitored contact.

There are some bad reasons for dating and a parent must assess whether any of these are in the mix. There is the trophy boyfriend thing—in other words your daughter needs a boyfriend in order to feel better about herself. More pernicious is the need some girls and boys have to exercise sexual attraction over someone, because they can.

There just might be some good reasons to say yes to a request for permission to date. A developing friendship needs some space to grow. This might just be 'the one'. And some Christian young couples work well together and encourage each other in their faith. But you know your child.

However, there are lots of good reasons to encourage a young person to wait and not to worry if there is nobody sending a Valentine:

- Time is on their side

- It is wrong to mess people about and break hearts

- There are temptations in the area of purity

- There are plenty of other goals to focus on at this time of their lives

- It is fun at this stage to develop a wide range of friends and to socialise in a group.

## 2. Pornography

Adolescents are interested in sex. There is a natural curiosity about it. Commercial interests have exploited this by making pictures of nudity and sexual acts easily available. This is not new but these days it is more accessible than the top shelf at the local newsagents. The following chapter will explore more thoroughly the navigation of internet hazards. Pornography is extremely addictive; that is why evil people are so persistent in finding a way to bait potential customers online. There are of course certain blocks that parents can put in but the most effective ones are the ones that come from the child himself—an awareness of the enemy (1 Peter 5:8), a respect for what God has made good (Hebrews 13:4), a desire to please God (1 Thessalonians 4:1–6) and a thought life which focuses on the excellent not the seedy (Philippians 4:8).

### 3. Masturbation

The non-Christian is commonly heard to say that this is not a problem. Some sex education programmes might even encourage it, along the lines that it doesn't harm anyone. But since it is generally associated with lust, it can hardly be something that a Christian would want to condone (Colossians 3:5). It also separates the sexual act from loving relationship and so is a long way from God's design. This is a secret thing and embarrassing to talk about but if you discover that your child has a weakness in this area, you need also to recognise that they themselves will probably feel guilty about it. You may be able to pray with them about it and reassure them that although their conscience is pointing them in the right direction, this is not the unforgiveable sin.

### 4. 'Mum, I think I'm gay'

True Freedom Trust, which is a Christian organisation which helps people who are struggling with same-sex attraction issues, informed me that rarely in their experience does such a statement come from the lips of a teenager. Typically it would be the admission of a young person in his or her twenties. But in the face of the legalisation of same-sex marriage, the unquestioned mantra that sexual orientation is about the way you are made and the rampant promotion of the gay lifestyle as a cool choice, sexual confusion amongst teenagers is set to rise. I unequivocally recommend True Freedom Trust as a resource for parents who face this issue.

A young person who is embracing a gay identity may be doing so for a number of reasons. Identity in general is an issue for teenagers: they are finding out who they are. Imagine a boy who doesn't fit in with the sporty, beer-drinking types and feels alienated from the majority of boys in his class. He might unconsciously be just longing to be part of an identifiable group and in some circles it is quite trendy to be gay. Lots of celebrities are gay. He might believe this is the way to go—there is an identity to be had. Or he might on some occasion have been aroused by the sight of another boy in the showers and he jumps to the conclusion that he is gay.

For girls it is less a sexual thing than a relational one. Adolescent girls can have strong emotional attachments to other girls—they are looking for someone to love. In the current climate that can lead them to identify themselves as gay. They feel very safe. They no longer have to be on the treadmill of wishing and hoping for a boyfriend.

Of course there may be all kinds of other factors in the background contributing to the general emotional insecurity which statistically has been shown to be a significant factor in gender confusion in young people: a history of abuse, a broken home and other kinds of dysfunction. Parents are sometimes all too aware of this and so their child's declaration is likely to engender guilt, whether real or imagined. Parents, taken by surprise, are often inclined to wonder 'How did I miss this?'

Recognise that, contrary perhaps to your expectation, you are not alone. There are no troubles in this world to which Christians are immune. This kind of thing happens sometimes to Christian parents. It nearly always comes as the most almighty shock and the response is like the response to a bereavement, which in a sense it is. There is grief, there is anger, there are doubts and questions and regrets and these things come in waves. But the stories I have read of people who have faced this is that it is really important, while not for one second backing down on what is the clear teaching of God's word, to remember that this is still your son or your daughter. Your child will already know what you think about it all and will expect you to cast them off. This is the time to come through with some recycled grace, remembering God's grace to you. Let them know that you love them as they are and even as they think they are. There is hope and a future (Jeremiah 29:11). God is able to use this painful circumstance in your life for your good and the good of your child.

## The big choice

Accept that your child will make his or her own mind up on where to go with love, sex and marriage. But the bigger and more important question is not about sexuality at all but will they follow Jesus. Obviously if they are saying no to Jesus they will have little reason to follow his views on sex and marriage. Remember as a Christian parent what your ultimate aim is and then you will know how to pray and how to respond.

## Some practical inferences and applications

1. Marriages have to be worked at. Sometimes lovely Christian parents are so focused on their children that they neglect each other. This is a tragic mistake which will do your children

no good at all. What will your child learn about marriage by looking at yours?

2. Teach your growing children about relationships. Social skills do not come naturally and at the present time there is a vacuum where there used to be universally accepted mores of interaction between friends and across the genders. There is plenty of ammunition for teaching in the book of Proverbs. Look at the Bible together and find out what it has to say on friendship using the references quoted in that section of this chapter.

## For further reading/resources

'Going out, marriage and sex' by Dr Chris Richards and Dr Liz Jones (Day One)

'Youth Bible Study Guide: Sexuality' by Chip and Helen Kendall (Authentic)

'Surviving Middle School' by Rick Bundschuh (Authentic)

The True Freedom Trust website: www.truefreedomtrust.co.uk

The Lovewise website: www.lovewise.org.uk

# Chapter 9

# Net gain or net loss

## Children and communications technology

*A little girl was asked by a relative whether she would like to be an astronaut when she grew up. She paused and then replied, 'Do they have mobile phones on the moon?'*

L ife without mobile phones—are you old enough to remember it? The liberty! The inconvenience!

According to Ofcom research in 2012, 90% of 15-year olds and 40% of 10-year olds own a mobile phone. There has been a year on year rise in those statistics with the age of first ownership coming down. The latest trend is to switch from mobile to smartphone. A Smartphone, such as iPhone and Blackberry, is a mobile on which you can access e-mail and surf the internet, among other clever tricks. 75% of 15-year olds own one of those. 12–15-year olds send an average of 193 texts a week. They spend as much time on the internet as they do watching television—on average seventeen hours a week on each.

You can waste a lot of time on the said internet uncovering statistics like the above. They make for a slightly disquieting read and not just to those with a general IT aversion. Unlike all the other chapters of this book, this one explores a concern common to most parents, believers and non-believers alike.

No one seriously disputes the many advantages of the advances in communication technology. These things are here to stay and are now an integral part of life as we know it. Nonetheless there are many parents who at times would like to take the computer, the iPhone, iPad, iPod and the games console and chuck them off the top of the BT Tower. There are worries about obesity and obsession, concerns about cost and time-wasting, and most of all the fear of online pornographers, predators and cyberbullies. In the light of some recent tragic cases the Prime Minister, David Cameron, suggested that the government might legislate to make filtering services mandatory for internet service providers (ISPs). These however would only offer protection on the network concerned. Your child might go next door ....

## Parent policing power

There is a lot of talk about parental controls and certainly there are software packages a parent can buy. These would serve to filter harmful content and monitor usage. But this software would only protect the device on which it was installed.

There are other things a parent can do to restrict how a device like a mobile phone can be used. A parent might disable the browser on the device but that would not prevent the child from installing and using an app which had its own embedded browser.

All this I learned in conversation with someone at church who is both a parent and a computer expert. He told me that when you access the internet there is usually a service called a Domain Name System (DNS). This is what locates the specific interest site the user is trying to access. Usually the DNS is provided by the ISP (internet service provider) but a parent can override this and use a third party DNS service (e.g. OpenDNS) instead. If this is done from your router it can provide a way to filter and monitor all internet traffic from your home.

But this same computer expert told me that ultimately there is always a way round these controls if a child is determined enough. And we all know how smart children can be with electronic devices. Also none of the above controls can protect a child once he or she has got onto a permitted site. One thing can lead to another and sometimes on a computer, as in life, you can find yourself where you did not initially intend to be.

## The danger of addiction

Protecting your child from some of the content is only part of the problem, there is the issue of time spent on these devices and the effect that may have. One of our children very much enjoyed computer games. My husband and I started to notice a difference in him when he had been playing a little while; he was more withdrawn, less connected to us. It was a warning to us to strictly limit his exposure.

According to BBC Panorama, December 2010, 24 million people in Britain play computer games. Half of the homes in Britain have a games console and of course many can be played via other devices too.

Computer games tend to be an immersive experience. Some children play for 12 hours at a time. There have been reports of youngsters playing continuously for 2 or 3 days without sleep to try to get to the next level.

The extraordinary graphics of the latest computer games are extremely compelling and addictive. They draw the player in and where played for long periods of time can lead to a tendency to substitute the virtual world for the real world. The World Health Organisation recognises this as a serious threat to the health of European youth.

It is not just games that are addictive. There is also concern among parents about the obsession their children apparently have with social network sites, checking and adjusting their profile many times a day. Almost half of British children aged 9–12 use social networking sites despite the minimum age requirement of 13.

Humans are vulnerable to addictions of all kinds because of that inner restlessness which is a result of the fall. Children, no less than adults, have a need to belong and a need to find an identity. Both of these needs are met in a relationship with Jesus Christ. Without him we are all looking for other solutions. An escape into a game where we are uncluttered with the complexities of real human relationships can make a child feel safe. And when it all goes wrong he can just switch it off. He is not obliged to face the long-term consequences of his actions.

Social network sites offer an even greater chance to create an identity, to be somebody, to belong to something and to feel very popular. The average number of Facebook 'friends' that a 12–15 year old has is 286, although bizarrely she will not have met 25% of those 'friends' in person.

To recognise the addictive potential of screen-time is important. But a Christian has a great deal more to offer this discussion than merely sharing concerns. Firstly, a Christian has a worldview which enables him to understand where the real problem lies; secondly a Christian is likely to have a greater clarity of vision about what things in cyber space are resolutely to be kept out there; thirdly a Christian parent will take seriously the responsibility of setting and maintaining boundaries, even where that makes him unpopular with his offspring; fourthly and most crucially, a Christian has something much better to offer.

## The source of evil

Technology, unlike say pornography, which we discussed in the last chapter, is morally neutral. Evil, as we have seen, comes from the human heart. Technological progress merely presents new channels for the same old stuff. In Jesus' day some of the religious people were concerned about the corruption and contamination caused by a failure to engage in ritual washing. Jesus put his disciples right with a fundamental statement about the human heart.

'But what comes out of the mouth proceeds from the heart, and this defiles a person. For out of the heart come evil thoughts, murder, adultery, sexual immorality, theft, false witness, slander. These are what defile a person.' Matthew 15:18–20

Jesus' list, quoted above, could very well be referring to the so called 'dangers of the internet'. But the threat comes from the people who use it, and that includes you and me.

## The virtue of self-control

The most valuable thing I learned from my computer-savvy friend was this: the only real protection has to come from within the child himself. Of course attempting to filter out harmful content is wise. Of course a parent should be vigilant over a child's online activities. But relying on simply turning on the controls and walking away is not going to work anymore than locking a kitchen drawer will prevent your child harming himself with sharp knives. There are knives in other places and he is sure to meet them sometime.

So once again in this book it comes down to training. Mere external controls only guarantee temporary safety. Self-control is what really protects. Children have to be taught to use the internet wisely and to say 'no' themselves to some things. That implies educating their taste and their discernment. This is much bigger than the internet. It includes all media, choice of friends, priorities and the path through life. It is about the heart.

'Keep your heart with all vigilance,
for from it flow the springs of life.'                    Proverbs 4:23

## The impact of words

Hannah Smith, aged 14, took her own life in August 2013 after online bullying via the social networking site ask.fm. The discussions that followed this tragedy centred on the policing of social networking sites which do not do enough to protect users from those who post unkind comments behind a cloak of anonymity.

But words come from people. Words have always been potentially lethal, as the Bible recognises.

'... but no human being can tame the tongue. It is a restless evil, full of deadly poison.'                                          James 3:8

One social network user spoke about chatting on the internet in this way: 'You become less conscious of the individuals involved, less inhibited, less embarrassed and less concerned about how you will be evaluated.' In other words the stopper is well and truly off the poison bottle. Undiluted venom is possible if you are in that kind of mood. It is so easy. There is no place for sensitivity in cyber-space.

We need to carefully teach our children about words and their effects.

## The honesty of face-to-face friendship

Cyber-bullying is easy because the bully does not have to face her victim and watch the effect. There are subtleties in social skills which are learned and which come into play only when you are in the bodily presence of the one you are talking to. Even the phone has its communication limitations but at least you have tone of voice to go on. Without that and the body language, and the visual response, and the eye-contact, and the physiology which accompanies a face-to-face encounter (blushing, sweating, heart-racing) a speaker just has words, typed onto a screen and fired off in an instant. Absolutely fine for the passing on of impersonal information, somewhat more dicey for the expressing of opinions, extremely dangerous for the sharing of intimate personal details with strangers or semi-strangers, but perfect for sounding off at random like a verbal scatter-gun. Ouch.

That is another thing about facebook 'friends'—they mostly aren't. And children need to be educated by their parents in the art of friendship as per the previous chapter. They also need to know that, as I heard one young person say, 'Nobody makes friends online; it's just a place to show them off.'

Creating a profile on facebook is a huge temptation to re-invent yourself as you would like to be or as you would like others to see you. To a generation brought up without the concept of living to please God it presents an opportunity to be a celebrity to a world-wide audience. You can airbrush out the bits of yourself you don't much like (And who will know?). You can put yourself at the centre of a multitude of friends and sell them a really upbeat version of your own life—or if not upbeat, coolly cynical or winsomely self-deprecating. But it doesn't have to be real. It is a projection onto a wall. That is all.

When the apostle John wrote his second and his third letters, both times he stressed the limitations of pen and ink and looked forward to real face-to-face communication.

'I had much to write to you, but I would rather not write with pen and ink. I hope to see you soon, and we will talk face to face,'

3 John: 13–14

Face to face is the essence of real communication in a real relationship. Moses was described as the friend of God because God spoke to him face to face (Deuteronomy 34:10; Exodus 33:11). In the priestly blessing (Numbers 6:24–26) the Lord turns 'his face towards you'. Initiating 'friendships' online should be strictly forbidden. It is a contradiction in terms.

## The importance of openness

Just as you would monitor the people who come in your front door, and how long they stay, and make sure they leave after a suitable time, so you will monitor internet use. Although portable devices make this difficult, you can at least restrict use of the computer to a public family area. That is a good tip for television as well. TVs in bedrooms are a very poor idea.

But openness is also a relationship thing. Try to keep family life a shared life. Some things are private, of course, but privacy should be more about modesty than secrecy. If a habit is developed of telling each other what you are doing and where you are going, then there will be routine accountability.

In the Bible secrecy is generally associated with being up to no good. Bring things into the light. Light exposes darkness and bad stuff exposed can be dealt with.

## The beauty of commitment

One of the things that many commentators are beginning to notice is that habitual use of texting is changing the way people look at commitment. Think back a decade or so if you can. You made an arrangement with your friend to meet for a coffee at a certain time and place one week hence. Amazingly you both showed up. This is how you organised your life by making arrangements and sticking to them. The texting generation does not operate quite like that. Because they assume instant contact they like to keep their options open; they tend to not make arrangements more than 24 hours ahead and when they do they continually adjust them. They change their plans several times a day as they receive new information and input it into their mental data base; every day is a shifting kaleidoscope of possibilities.

This affects mutual trust and therefore relationships. With such a fluid attitude the only person's needs worth considering are one's own right now. Everybody is working their world to suit themselves. It is a long way from that underrated virtue, faithfulness, and the kind of commitment-keeping commended by the promise-keeping God. In Psalm 15 one of the marks of godliness is the one 'who swears to his own hurt and does not change' (Psalm 15:4).

As Christian parents teach their children about the God who is always faithful to his word, and as they aim to keep their own promises even when it is inconvenient, so they should expect their children to stick to their commitments. Words are binding. A verbal contract is a contract. If you said you would do it, do it.

## The pleasures in simplicity

The Australian writer and journalist, Susan Maushart, observed with some frustration that her three teenage children were spending every waking minute, including some when they should have been asleep, tuned into some kind of electronic device, so she decided to pull the plug, literally. The family spent six months without any of it—iPod, computer, phone, even TV. It was a kind of technological detox. Needless to say they all found it hard. Susan Maushart has described the experience in her book 'The Winter of our Disconnect' (2011). She records that despite the strops and the moods during that time the family rediscovered each other and also some simple pleasures, like singing together.

Perhaps the greatest danger of TV and internet use is the time it swallows of children lives. It makes them fat and unfit, dulls their minds, reduces their attention span and robs them of independence, creativity, adventure and companionship.

There is a world out there to explore. Any parent who believes that God has made a beautiful world should be encouraging their children to get out and explore it, even if it is only with a rusty old bike, a kite made of a binbag or chalked out hopscotch squares. When weather and darkness keeps you indoors get stuck into making, baking, music, drama, board games, painting, balsa-wood modelling etc., etc., etc.

There are also people out there to be with, to know, to love and to serve. The isolating effect of screen activity means that children are growing up less practised in the art of getting along together. They are better at making phony non-friends on screen than they are at making friends with a living, breathing, human child who lives next door. Today's children need lots of practice in relating. They cannot learn that from a screen.

Of course children are all different. There have always been geeks and we love them. In the old days they would have been train-spotting or stamp-collecting. Shy and socially awkward as such children can be, the screen presents them with an ideal safe setting for their lives. But make them wise to the dangers of too much and build some diversity into their lives.

## Screen Hygiene

While a wise parent recognises the limitations of external controls, it makes sense to set some boundaries and guidelines for your children's interface with screens of various kinds. These form part of your training. A parent should follow them too and thereby model her own strictly controlled use of electronic media. At the end of Susan Maushart's book, she gives a list of eleven commandments for keeping a sane and healthy balance between the need to use modern technology and enjoy it and remembering that it is not real life. Here are some of them:

Thou shalt not fear boredom

Thou shalt not 'multitask' (not until thy kingdom come, thy homework be done)

Thou shalt keep the Sabbath a screen-free day

Thou shalt keep thy bedroom a media-free zone

Thou shalt not covet thy neighbour's upgrade

Thou shalt bring no media to thy dinner

Thou shalt bring no dinner to thy media

You might want to adopt some of those for your own family code.

## Something better

Any parent, especially a modern one, would like to do more than be negative. In addition to limiting screen time and encouraging other non-electronic activities, a Christian wants to introduce her children to things which have real significance. Computer games and facebook profiles don't mean a thing. They may give some temporary pleasure but in the long-term they do not enrich or enhance the child's life or anyone else's. Encourage them to think bigger, or even, if like David they sometimes contemplate the stars, to think smaller.

'When I look at your heavens, the work of your fingers,
the moon and the stars, which you have set in place,
what is man that you are mindful of him,
and the son of man that you care for him? ... O Lord, our Lord, how
majestic is your name in all the earth!'                    Psalm 8:3, 4, 9

## Some practical inferences and applications

1. How much time per week are your children spending in front of a screen? Keep a log to find out if it is really too much. Are there any evidences of obsession or addiction?

2. Review your child's social skills. Is it time for some input or some practice? Throw a party. Invite the neighbours in.

## For further reading

'You, your family and the internet' by David Clark (Day One)

'Will you be my Facebook Friend?' by Tim Chester

# Chapter 10

# Spend, spend, spend

## The perils of living in an affluent society

*Two young boys were discussing what they would do if they won the lottery. They were good friends. One said to the other, 'If I won a million pounds I would give you half.'*

*'What if you won half a million?' said his friend.*

*'Yes I'd give you half,' was the answer.*

*'What about quarter of a million.'*

*'Yes of course.'*

'*What about a thousand?*'

'*Yes.*'

'*Five hundred?*'

'*Yes.*'

'*Would you give me half of fifty pounds?*'

'*Yes.*'

'*What about if you had one pound?*'

'*That's not fair! You know I've got one pound!*'

Too often discussions about money can be academic. We can be very wise and generous about what we haven't got.

People in the western world tend to consider that what they have got is not quite enough. Whether they earn £20,000 or £200,000 per annum they frequently believe that they could do with about a third more. That is according to research quoted by the psychologist Oliver James in his 2007 book 'Affluenza'. He was interested in finding out causes of depression and anxiety and identified what he called a virus which has spread across the globe. He calls this virus 'affluenza'. Symptoms of this virus include:

- Aspirations to wealth

- Aspirations to fame

- Wanting to hide the signs of ageing

- Love of admiration

- Obsession with fashion

- Needing to be complimented on appearance

- Tendency to compare what you have with what others have got

- Preoccupation with shopping

- Measuring success in life by what you own

- Believing that your life would be improved if you owned certain things you don't have

- Less concerned with work than what you can do with what you get for it

Even after a cursory glance at that list the reader will be unsurprised to learn that Oliver James found the virus to be rampant. He also linked it to an increasing susceptibility to the commonest emotional diseases such as anxiety and depression.

We live in a society where the symptoms described above are

commonplace to the point of being unquestioned. These are not symptoms, they are twenty-first century values. Andrew Marr, in his TV documentary series on modern Britain made the same point about the cultural shift since the early nineties, drawing attention to the public obsession with possessions, appearances and fame. Shopping malls are the new cathedrals. Shopping is the new national sport. It is what people chiefly do with their weekends. Witness the hordes returning to the multi-storey car parks in towns and cities all over the UK loaded with bulging carrier bags, week after week.

How does that affect the raising of children? The obvious answer is that parents spend a fortune on their children in the belief that buying them stuff will make them happy. That is why there is 7.2 billion pounds of stuff in British children's bedrooms. 36 billion Lego bricks are manufactured every year, and marketed at high prices. Since Lego bricks are practically indestructible and they have been on the market for over 50 years, one wonders where they all are. Somebody did the maths and worked out that if all the Lego bricks ever made were distributed equally amongst the population of the whole world, every single person would have 62 bricks. You don't need stupid maths like that to recognise that there are a lot of toys out there, and since they are not distributed equally amongst the world's population, a smaller number of children have an awful lot of them, and a load of other stuff as well.

One of the greatest pressures parents tell me that they feel is the pressure to buy. One mother spoke to me about the difficulty of taking her daughter into shops because she always asked for things. Some parents almost feel that they have to prove they are good parents by getting hold of this year's most desired toy for their offspring. Others are subject to flagrant manipulation, truly believing that they have to buy certain makes of trainers, bags or other items for their children to prevent them being bullied.

Possessions are important in our day and age because they confer an identity. And in particular it is the label on a given possession which grants status. That is why, where once manufacturers' labels were discreetly tucked away on a garment, they are now emblazoned, even writ large for all the world to see. It is not just a sweatshirt, it is a Gap sweatshirt and that information can be read at fifty paces. To buy a product with the right label is to buy into being a certain kind of person. Children are well tuned into this before they leave primary school. They rate each other by their stuff.

Does this matter to a Christian? Should we just not worry and, as long as we are not getting into debt, join in the party? Some of you know your Bibles a little too well to be quite at home in the current ethos. Let us remind ourselves about what the Bible teaches about money.

## Everything belongs to God

'The earth is the Lord's and the fullness thereof,
the world and those who dwell therein.'                    Psalm 24:1

Ultimately this whole world is God's, because he made it. Humans are to be stewards of his creation. It is true that their labour produces wealth but it is God who gives the ability to work and to earn.

'Beware lest you say in your heart, "My power and the might of my hand have gotten me this wealth." You shall remember the Lord your God, for it is he who gives you power to get wealth, ...'

Deuteronomy 8:17–18

## God expects people to live productive lives

Honest labour is to be the means of creating wealth. Adam was put into the garden to work (Genesis 2:15) and to enjoy the fruits of his labour (Genesis 2:16). Laziness is a sin (Proverbs 10:4).

There is a legitimate satisfaction in work and the wealth it creates. God confirms the right to the ownership of property in the eighth commandment: 'You shall not steal.' And he wants us to make the connection between work and wealth (Proverbs 14:23–24).

## The uses of wealth

The purpose of work in the Bible is to be useful, not to confer status. It is quite normal in our society to assess people by their occupation and to be more impressed by a doctor than a postman, but this is quite unscriptural. The usefulness of work is in the service it provides to others and in the provision we make for ourselves and our dependants.

Money generated by our work is therefore first and foremost to house, feed and clothe ourselves and our families (1 Timothy 5:8). Prudent foresight will lead us to plan and budget carefully, to ensure that what we have will cover our needs until the next payday (Proverbs 21:20). There is also a recognition in the Bible of the right to pass on wealth to your children (Proverbs 19:14).

But that is not the only use of wealth. When Paul wrote to the Ephesians about what a life transformed by the Holy Spirit looks like, he included a direction for the converted burglar:

'Let the thief no longer steal, but rather let him labour, doing honest work with his own hands, so that he may have something to share with anyone in need.'                    Ephesians 4:28

The taker, post conversion, would become a worker and a giver. So we learn that money generated by work is to be shared around a bit outside the immediate family. There have always been inequalities in wealth. But the Biblical principle is: the more you have, the more you are accountable for and the more you give away. That was the idea behind the ten per cent tithing system in the Old Testament, started by Abraham (Genesis 14:20) and restated in the instructions to the redeemed people of God before they entered the Promised Land (Deuteronomy 14:22). New Testament believers also gave as they were able and beyond (2 Corinthians 8:3). Paul's instruction to rich Christians via the young pastor Timothy was:

'They are to do good, to be rich in good works, to be generous and ready to share.'                    1 Timothy 6:18

The principle is to honour God with your wealth (Proverbs 3:9), recognising the initial point which is that everything belongs to him anyway. When we give our tenth, we only give our due; we are not doing anything amazing. When we are privileged to be able to give more we are laying up treasure in heaven (1 Timothy 6:19; Matthew 6:20).

## Fortress or prison?

The Bible does not deny that there is a certain security in having money in the bank (Proverbs 10:15). But that security can also be a snare, leading idolatrous people in every generation since time began to imagine that they can do without God. Who needs God when you have money? Sadly that has been precisely the thinking in many nations of the affluent, secular West, just as it was in Old Testament Israel to their detriment and downfall. Not only is this the most outrageous act of treason, it sends people on a fruitless quest of always looking for soul satisfaction in the wrong place. That is why Paul prefaces his remarks about how rich people should use their wealth with a salutary reminder about the limits of what money can do.

> 'As for the rich in this present age, charge them not to be haughty, nor to set their hopes on the uncertainty of riches, but on God, who richly provides us with everything to enjoy.' 1 Timothy 6:17

Wealth is uncertain. That is true in this life as recent history has shown. But it is of absolutely no value at the day of judgment (Proverbs 11:4). That is why we should not put our hope in it. But Paul's other point is that real pleasure comes in another place. Not only is a believer's security in God, a believer's joy is in God. Does God want us to be miserable? Not at all! He himself is a happy and generous God. And he wants us to experience the immense delight of knowing him in Christ, 'in whom are hidden all the treasures of wisdom and knowledge' (Colossians 2:3).

## The contented Christian

Paul, writing from prison to the Philippian church, said he had discovered the secret of contentment.

'I know how to be brought low, and I know how to abound. In any and every circumstance, I have learned the secret of facing plenty and hunger, abundance and need. I can do all things through him who strengthens me.'                    Philippians 4:12–13

This contentment is an inward thing, so different from the 'I must have that to be happy' ethos of contemporary society. Contentment is a matter of the heart. Paul has already written of the peace of God in his heart; he has already spoken of his ultimate, all-consuming passion and ambition to know Christ better. It was his inner communion with Christ which enabled him to transcend his personal circumstances. He could enjoy possessions when he had them but he hung loose to them; when he didn't have them he could be equally happy. Knowing Christ made all the difference.

I frequently visit my elderly mother-in-law. She is wearing several layers of clothes and a double blanket over her knees. She says she needs them to keep warm. I look out of the window. Across the road in the park there are children playing wearing only t-shirts and shorts. The Puritan Jeremiah Burrows who wrote about 'the rare jewel of Christian contentment' said the world's idea of contentment is like an old person keeping warm—she needs lots of layers. But the contentment of a Christian is like the warmth of children. They do not need lots of layers because they are warm from within. There is a strong inner vitality generating warmth to their bodies. God's children can know that inner warmth of contentment.

If contentment was rare in Puritan times, I am guessing it is rarer now. What an opportunity for witness this presents to the Christian family! My husband in his 1999 book 'Christians in a Consumer Culture' wrote about 'the shocking impact of a contented Christian'. When the whole world is living for money and possessions and talking about moving to a bigger house, getting a better car, saving for one home improvement after another, would not a person who refused to get on that particular treadmill raise a few eyebrows? You could decide not to trade in the old model for a better one. You could refuse to upgrade the children's bikes/computers/bedroom furniture. So many of our 'going against the tide' issues might tend to make us unpopular or downright peculiar. But being counter-cultural in this way might also have its attractive aspect. It has some ecological brownie points from the point of view of not wanting to use up more than necessary of the earth's resources. And Christians who stand out against waste and greed are in line with Bible principles. But the ultimate motivation is not to do with this world but the next, of which every Christian is a citizen. Perhaps if your difference attracted attention you might have opportunity to speak humbly of the source of your contentment.

Sadly, I fear, too many of us have been infected with the affluenza virus. There is absolutely no point in wondering why our children are so materialistic without looking at ourselves and wondering whether we have passed on this extremely contagious disease. This is an ongoing challenge for us all. We are so accustomed to materialism we barely notice the inroads it has made into our thinking.

The Bible's way of getting rid of bad habits is to replace them with good ones. This is not a matter of mere resolution, but of humbling yourself, drawing near to God and asking his inward renewal day by day. (James 4:4–10).

Good habits can be translated into family routines and family policy. These, again, do not replace inward change, but they do affect mindset and character of a growing child more than you might think. They also offer some guidelines and boundaries.

## Principles to model and teach

### 1. Gratitude

'And be thankful ... with thankfulness in your hearts to God ... giving thanks to God the Father ...'          Colossians 3:15–17

Three times in as many verses Paul stresses the thread of thankfulness as an integral part of the clothing of a Christian. It is so much easier to notice what doesn't suit. It is so easy to take for granted the ordinary goodies that come to us with the regularity of the sunrise. A thankful spirit makes you feel much better and it is contagious.

Being thankful is different from saying 'thank you' but the latter place is somewhere to start. That early training of your children is worth the hassle. And even though you know they are merely parroting the words as a kind of password, do not retreat. I know some families who also train their children to add, after the mandatory 'thank you', a sentence beginning with the words 'I particularly liked ...' e.g. 'I particularly liked the blackcurrant drink/the picture on the wall.' That might in some cases be pushing insincerity beyond the bounds of reasonable endurance, and can be relentlessly parodied and trivialised, but it is a practice designed to make children think. Certainly it is something a parent could model in a sincere expression of thanks. And in reviewing at bedtime prayers the joys of the day just spent, explicit appreciation far surpasses the cliché of the blanket 'Thank you for all the nice things of today'.

This whole strand is not just about thanking people for the things they give, which is a matter of good manners. That, of course, is really important. But beyond that it is about acknowledging God the Father as the generous giver, of recognising the good hand of his providence which governs our lives, It is a way of seeing the world—a worldview. And it will come out in the frequency with which you find yourself saying, 'Isn't God kind! ... I am so thankful ... Thank you, Lord.'

This is an antidote to moaning, self-pity and always wanting more. Recognise what has already graciously been given.

## 2. Simplicity

'Consider the lilies of the field, how they grow.'   Matthew 6:28

In a high-tech, over-priced world it is good to regularly take delight in small and simple things. This is also an antidote to internet addiction as we observed in the previous chapter. Children are very sensual—encourage them to use their senses, even quite separately, to take in the smell of baking bread, the sound of birdsong, the colours of the sky. When I started primary school teaching, the nature table was a feature of every classroom. Now sadly it has made way for high-tech teaching aids. Why not have a nature table at home? I was frequently astonished by the immense delight our children took in sticks. They rarely returned from a country walk without one. Never underestimate the fascination of the simplest of objects.

Apart from the pleasures provided in the beautiful world God has made, there are social pleasures of interacting with people— even chance encounters with people in the park or over the fence. The spectre of stranger danger can cause us to teach our children to mistrust and suspect everybody and in some cases has driven parents to direct their children to the perceived comparative safety of solitary interaction with an expensive toy. That is a huge loss all round. Of course you have to be wise but an honest and cheerful connection with others is a simple joy which cannot be bought with money.

In other words, as far as possible, replace pseudo experiences with real ones. And when it comes to buying things refuse resolutely to pander to label obsession. If you start it, you make it harder to break. A pair of trainers is a pair of trainers. Do not confuse quality with name. There may sometimes be a case to be made that 'you get what you pay for', but be careful about automatic assumptions. Especially, do not encourage a status identity linked to stuff. It is false and shallow. Frankly your children are better off without the kind of 'friends' who only rate others by their possessions. Don't be afraid to tell them that. God looks on the heart. We do not have his view of things but where the heart is exposed it gives us all a good pointer.

### 3. Moderation

'give me neither poverty nor riches;
feed me with the food that is needful for me,
lest I be full and deny you

and say, "Who is the Lord?"
or lest I be poor and steal
and profane the name of my God.'                    Proverbs 30:7–9

There is a wise balance in that verse which was a help to me in raising my children. You don't have to go to extremes. You are not called upon to be miserly and miserable and only ever get the bare minimum. That might lead to bitterness, envy and resentment. But you don't have to be lavish either, even if you could afford to be. Take the spending down a notch by choosing something cheaper from the menu.

A moderate attitude will help us to avoid going nuts when we buy presents for our children. It is fun to buy a marvellous toy but it unhelpful and unwise to raise our children's expectations and indeed their sense of entitlement. Overloading them with stuff can actually devalue the presents they receive and diminish the pleasure of receiving.

## 4. Generosity

'Be generous and you will be prosperous; help others and they will help you'.

That was one of our family mottos, a paraphrase of Proverbs 11:25, written up and framed on the wall. One of our children in adulthood told me that it had had a profound effect upon him. Another Christian told us that a lasting memory of his childhood was the frequent sight of parcels piled up in the hall, waiting to be posted to missionaries serving overseas. His parents just couldn't stop giving.

We have a generous God and his image-bearers reflect him more brightly when they are generous. One of the great unsung pleasures of life is giving and Christian parents will want to build into their children's lives the opportunity of discovering that. However little or much God has given you, there are opportunities to share if you look around.

If you have a home and a table and food, offer hospitality and involve your children in this, either in the guest list, the cooking, the serving or the entertaining.

If you have a spare seat in your car, whom could you invite to join you on an outing?

If you have outgrown clothes or toys, who could benefit?

The second half of the Proverbs verse was also true for us as a family when we were the recipients of the cast-offs of others. Our children loved nothing better than 'a bag'.

I was very impressed by a family I knew where the children were encouraged to make lists at Christmas, not of what they hoped to get, but of what they intended to give. Certainly that season of the year is a huge snare for children. But it can be turned round as an object lesson in the pleasures of giving as we celebrate the gift of the Saviour.

Giving money is a delicate subject because there is a sense in which they don't own anything until they are earning. Some parents give pocket money but along with it strict expectations of tithing into the collection at church. That can become more like a tax and not quite in the secret, voluntary and cheerful giving recommended by Scripture. So other parents prefer to suggest rather than command, and then mind their own business.

## The grandparent factor

Many Christian parents I have met would agree with all of the above then find themselves frustrated by the activities of 'spoiling Granny'. This can be a tricky one to handle because you don't want to jeopardise either your children's relationship with their grandparents or your own with your parents, especially where there are in-laws involved. Every situation is different but here are some things I have learned and which I have observed in others who manage this well.

Firstly, the Bible teaches us to honour our parents. That means that we recognise the unique place they have in our lives. While we have left home and started our own families, these are people whose sacrificial care for us in the past and love for us in the present deserves our respect, at the very least. It is right that our children should have regular and warm contact with their living forebears. If you have misgivings, don't publicise them to the children.

'Grandchildren are the crown of the aged,
and the glory of children is their fathers.'          Proverbs 17:6

Secondly, we should remember that the relationship is different. Grandparents are frequently heard to remark that the great thing about grandchildren is that you hand them back. Children also recognise the difference and they sometimes manage it much better than their parents. Because a grandparent relationship is one stage removed, grandparents don't have to do exactly as parents would do. Our children loved the fact that at Nanny's the Coca-cola was on tap, there was a cupboard stuffed to the gunnels with sweets and the TV was always on. At times it wound us the parents up until we relaxed and stopped being po-faced killjoys. Grandparents delight to do things for their grandchildren that they couldn't, due to more straitened circumstances, have done for their grandchildren's parents. It's a short-term thing and its effects are short-lived too. Our children knew better than to expect or ask for the same things at home. That is what made going to see Nanny and Grandad so special. So don't be defensive and think that you are looking like mean Mum and Dad in comparison to the bounty elsewhere. Let the grandparents be grandparents, not surrogate parents. Unless in fact they are.

Thirdly, if you have a spoiling Granny in the background, factor it in. Perhaps it means that you can cut down your own spending at Christmas and birthdays to prevent overload. Perhaps it means you can have a helpful chat with your parents, liberally overlaid with appreciation, to divert some of the money in the direction of sensible or necessary items, or towards an outing rather than things.

Fourthly, always emphasise both to your children, your parents and yourselves the value of the non-material things grandparents offer. How wonderful to have other people to whom your children are special in a unique way. That kind of love is worth more to your children than a lump sum in an ISA. The sense of history and belonging which accompany extended family is also beyond price. Explore and appreciate that.

Finally, if you are blessed with Christian parents, and therefore your children with Christian grandparents, keep them regularly updated with the real lowdown about your children for their prayers. This is perhaps the most excellent of all grandparently offices: to pray. Invite them to do this and thank them when they do. Parents need all the help they can get.

## Some practical inferences and applications

1. 'You have multiplied, O Lord my God,
   your wondrous deeds and your thoughts toward us;
   none can compare with you!
   I will proclaim and tell of them,
   yet they are more than can be told.' Psalm 40:5

   God's wonders are too many to declare, but the old-fashioned exercise of counting your blessings is a tried and tested way out of self-pity and avarice. Have a go and make it a regular practice, both by yourself and as a family.

2. Some of the stuff that finds its way into our homes is an invitation to discontent and covetousness. From weekend supplements to discount stores catalogues, check out if they are serving any useful purpose. If not, have a purge.

## For further reading

'Christians in a Consumer Culture' by John Benton (Christian Focus)

'The Busy Christian's Guide to Busyness' by Tim Chester (IVP)

## Chapter 11

# Is it indoctrination?

## Fearlessly passing on the baton of truth

'We've decided not to send Harry along to that Holiday Club at your church this year,' said Debbie to her fellow-parent Rhona at the school gate.

'Oh?' responded Rhona in surprise, 'He had such a good time last year.'

'Yes he loved the games. But it was all those Bible verses and stories about Jesus. Adam and I have decided we want Harry to make up his own mind on these things when he is older. We ourselves are neutral on these matters. We don't want him brainwashed.'

**M**any secular parents in Britain today are quite proud of the fact that, unlike evangelical Christians of their acquaintance, they do not engage in indoctrination. Such comments as Debbie's to Rhona, quoted above, can make a Christian parent wobble. Should we back off on the Bible stories? Should we soft pedal the Scripture songs?

## The myth of neutrality

The first thing we need to be clear about is that nobody, but nobody, is neutral on these matters. Challenge that ridiculous idea wherever you meet it. Every parent, every person, has a view on spiritual things. Debbie and Adam are proud of their neutrality, but if refusing your child permission to hear about Jesus is neutral, I'm a flower fairy. Their 'neutrality' is an emphatic stance for secular, atheistic materialism and it will come through loud and clear to Harry through every similar choice and decision his parents make.

So no Christian should tremble at such empty rhetoric.

What is it that Adam and Debbie really fear?

## The power of truth claims

One of the big headlines in the post-modern world (which is the world which like it or not we all inhabit) is that truth is personal. It is not out there, it is in here i.e. in the person who believes it. Therefore your non-Christian friend may be truly delighted that you have a faith, but that has nothing to do with him. And if you should try at any point to persuade him, he is likely to be either totally impervious or quite angry. For the post-modernist mindset believes that all truth-claims are a power play to control someone else's life; therefore they should rightly be ditched or at least privatised: 'How dare you challenge my right to believe what I want to?'

Many people have spotted the illogicality of the post-modern position and have expressed it more ably than I will, but it comes down to this. The statement 'there is no absolute truth' is itself a truth claim. So the argument self-destructs. But the assumption remains. 'I am neutral; you are biased; she is downright brainwashed.'

## Indoctrination v teaching

There is however a difference between indoctrination and teaching and the Bible is clear that what Christians should engage in is the latter not the former. Here are some points of distinction:

- Indoctrination lets its subjects into only some of the information—the rest is guarded and in the hands of an elite. Teaching is opening a door to everything, with nothing to hide.

- Indoctrination forbids questions. Teaching thrives on questions as the route to learning more.

- Indoctrination works on its subjects to make them unresisting to the message, by means for example of tiring them out, or weakening their will or working solely at the emotional level. Teaching on the other hand never bypasses the mind but seeks to engage it.

The apostle Paul is an example of one who taught. Yes, he proclaimed the truth but he did it by means of discussion, argument and reason. See, for example Acts 19:8–10. And he famously instructed those saved by God's mercy to 'be transformed by the renewal of your mind' (Romans 12:2). Luke begins his gospel by commending careful investigation (Luke 1:1–4). The Christian faith is eminently reasonable.

So when it comes to passing on the baton of truth to our children, which, as we shall see, certainly falls within the job description of a parent, we know at once that we are not in the business of forcing a mantra on our children or of making assumptions about them. We will teach them; we will engage their developing minds. This will be in keeping with Paul's command in Ephesians 6:4:

> 'Fathers, do not provoke your children to anger, but bring them up in the discipline and instruction of the Lord.'

## Passing on the baton

When Moses was on the very edge of the promised land with his new generation Israelites, he reiterated to them God's expectations of them in the book we know as Deuteronomy—second law. He was aware that they would be living in a unique way, very much against the tide of the surrounding nations. In fact, that was the point: they were to live in a distinctive way, not just because it was the best way to live, but because they were to show God to the world. As keepers of God's revelation about himself, they were to live it and pass it on to the succeeding generations so that God's name and his ways, as well as his line, would not vanish from the earth.

So, as believers in the Lord Jesus Christ, who have been let into 'God's mystery, which is Christ' (Colossians 2:2), we have a responsibility not only to live in Christ's ways before a watching pagan world, but also to guard the gospel (2 Timothy 1:14) and pass it on to others intact, not least to the next generation. In facing the challenge of passing on the baton of truth in our very secular culture, we have much to learn from Moses' words to the Israelites in Deuteronomy 6.

> 'Now this is the commandment—the statutes and the rules—that the Lord your God commanded me to teach you, that you may do them in the land to which you are going over, to possess it, that you may fear the Lord your God, you and your son and your son's son, by keeping all his statutes and his commandments, which I command you, all the days of your life, and that your days may be long. Hear therefore, O Israel, and be careful to do them, that it may go well with you, and that you may multiply greatly, as the Lord, the God of your fathers, has promised you, in a land flowing with milk and honey.'                                    Deuteronomy 6:1–3

Verses 1–4 spell it out. As the people enter the land they are to 'be careful' (v.3) not only to walk in God's ways themselves but to have an eye to the future—their children and their grandchildren (v.2).

The foundation of the teaching is summed up in verse 4.

> 'Hear, O Israel: The Lord our God, the Lord is one.'

This is the situation: God is there. There is one God, our loving creator and redeemer, eternally perfect, self-existent and self-sufficient. When we teach our children that, and live that, we are declaring simply what is the case.

No Bible-believing Christian would deny that Christianity is a truth-claim. That is the wonderful thing about it. The truth is out there. You didn't make it up. It is truth 'unchanged, unchanging', about an eternal, self-existent God. People may not like it at some points, but that won't make it go away.

## Our duty

'You shall love the Lord your God with all your heart and with all your soul and with all your might.'                                      v. 5

We are to love this God with a sincere love, a strong love, a superlative love. Matthew Henry in his commentary defines the love of God in the following way: 'be well pleased with him, desire that he may be ours and delight in contemplation of him and communion with him.' Note that the people are told to do this themselves as a prerequisite to teaching their children. If we do not, we are very likely to drop the baton of truth, because we are not gripping it tightly enough ourselves. What we have to pass on is not just a matter of fact or doctrine, but a passion. Where it fails to be so, we should not be surprised if our children let it go.

## Seven Top Tips from Deuteronomy 6

### 1. Think about it

'And these words that I command you today shall be on your heart.'                                                                          v. 6

It might sound obvious, but the more we think about God's

word, the better we will be at passing it on. I have a husband who loves football and three sons who do the same. My daughter and I were sometimes astonished at the ability of the four of them to recall, describe, dissect and analyse a detail of a match which took place months, even years ago. How could they do that? Answer: because in the meantime they thought about it a lot. I might sometimes see one of them deep in thought and ask what was on his mind? Perhaps I hoped that he was pondering some serious life issue, but it was generally whether the formation in such and such a match would have been better 4–4–2. My boys thought about football a lot.

Imagine how good we could be at talking, not to mention living, the gospel if we thought about it more, if our minds went to it in our spare moments. I often say to my Sunday school teaching team: 'there is no substitute for preparation.' Meditation on God's word is the best possible preparation for sharing it.

## 2. Teach it

'teach them diligently to your children.'                                    v. 7

The verb 'to teach diligently', according to the margin of my King James Bible, is from the Hebrew 'to whet or to sharpen'. I love the idea of sharpening up the minds of our children through Scripture truth. Again, note how far this is from indoctrination. It might be helpful to think about what is the content of this instruction and how parents might engage in it. Not everyone is a natural-born teacher. There are other places in the Bible which give us clues as to the curriculum for a growing child. It should include teaching about:

- The nature of God (Psalm 145:3–7). Introduce your children to God. With young children this can be done through Bible stories. You want your children to be thoroughly well-versed in these. The safest application is always along the lines of 'what do we learn about God here?' Although the stories also give us examples to follow and warnings about what to avoid (1 Corinthians 10:11) we need to be careful with these, lest our children learn to treat all of Scripture in a moralistic way.

- The way of salvation (2 Timothy 3:15). Since Timothy was taught from infancy by his believing mother and grandmother, we should not be afraid to teach our children the gospel, the main points of which are that God made us, we sinned, Jesus came to rescue us, we must trust in him. A young child can begin on systematic theology via a simple catechism. As young parents we used a song version of a children's catechism. To liven up family prayers, I invented a story about an engine who went off the rails and used it to teach Bible doctrine point by point. Paul includes in his list of 'elementary truths' (Hebrews 5:12; 6:1–2) such subjects as repentance, faith, baptism, the last things and judgment. So parents should cover the ground not just stick with stories which dumb down or make twee the great teachings of the Bible.

- The whole Bible story. I referred in chapter 2 to the meta-narrative of the Bible—the whole big picture of God's purposes in the world. This gives a sense of Biblical theology, as opposed to systematic theology and children need both. In fact a growing child will enjoy following the thread through Scripture of God's covenant plan and his redemptive purposes. Many psalms take this overview approach to meditate and adore God (see Psalm 105, 106, 107).

- How to live to please God. Obviously that is the immediate context of Deuteronomy 6. But Proverbs expands on it in a way that is very accessible to children. Proverbs 6:16–19 is explicit about what God does not like; Proverbs 6:6–11 address the sin of laziness; Proverbs 6:20–35 gives some well-grounded sex education. It is excellent especially with older children to get very practical.

The implication of impressing these things on your children is that within your daily family routines you make time for God. Call it what you like; do it when it suits—at breakfast, after supper, in bed—but as in all aspects of child-rearing, routines are your friend: routines for hygiene, routines for bedtime help establish certain things as given, as unquestioned. That is what you want with your Bible reading: a regular routine where expectations are clear.

So start young and start small but establish a pattern which you can maintain. Whether it is after breakfast, or after tea or at bedtime is entirely up to you. We had a short family time at the end of breakfast and individual Bible-reading and prayer with our children at bedtime. Eventually the bedtime routine was something that they took on independently. A habit was established which it was left to them to maintain. Your family life may call for something different. The important thing is that a non-negotiable routine is established.

My advice about how you conduct these times is that you keep in mind these three watchwords: short, lively, age-appropriate,

- Short! It is good to be short because then it won't become an intolerable burden to you or your child. Leave them wanting more with an 'awwww!' when you say 'and we'll hear more about that tomorrow!'

- Lively! With little children, tell stories, use props, or pictures. There are some excellent children's Bibles. Some have exquisite illustrations, some are very thorough and faithful to the Bible story. Some are particularly good at showing what the whole Bible is about. You might teach and sing songs which help the child to remember a story or some teaching. You might use other books which help children understand what the Bible is teaching e.g. *Pilgrim's Progress*. You might engage in learning some verses of Scripture together e.g. the ten commandments, Psalm 1; Psalm 23. Proverbs 6. Matthew 5. Lively means that although you are in a routine you are not in a rut.

- Age appropriate. As your children grow, you need to mature with them and adapt. As I implied earlier, there is a time when you will be backing off and leaving them to discover independently the joy of reading the Bible for themselves. There are various Bible-reading notes you can buy to train them in this.

## 3. Talk about it

'talk of them when you sit in your house, and when you walk by the way, and when you lie down, and when you rise.'

Do not box God up into your family prayer times and then carry on as if he was not there. You can talk about God anytime, not in a forced and artificial way but simply because he is a part of all of life. Surely many of those (slightly bizarre to us) ritual laws we find in Leviticus about fringes on garments and gardening and cooking were there to remind God's people that they are his people in the bedroom and the kitchen and the garden. He is the God of our whole lives. He has a view on just about everything. That does not mean you have to bring him into every conversation but it might be helpful to let his point of view pop up occasionally.

As our children got into their teens we found that conversations at mealtimes about news, current events and media often led to sparky conversations ranging over theology, different worldviews and the Christian life. Make the most of those.

The current equivalent of walking along the road might be when riding in the car. Again this can be a really good time for talking on serious things, especially when you are one-to-one with a teenager. But with younger children a good set of CDs to play and sing along to can both make the journey pass happily while every one learns something. Colin Buchanan has done Christian families a great service with his prodigious output of songs for children.

## 4. Take it in

'You shall bind them as a sign on your hand, and they shall be as frontlets between your eyes. You shall write them on the doorposts of your house and on your gates.'          v. 8-9

The custom, still observed by some orthodox Jews of having little boxes attached to head, wrist and door-frames comes from this verse. Surely God was meaning that God's word should be frequently ingested. The Israelites lived before printing but they were to remember that God has revealed himself in his written word. And to put it bluntly, if Almighty God has bothered to write it, we should take time frequently to read it, meditate on it and learn it.

With all our printed Bibles and other excellent aids to reading and understanding it, how seriously are we taking our Bible reading? Do our children sometimes catch us at it? Do they know there are times when we are not to be disturbed because we are reading and praying? If they do, they will understand how crucially central God's word is.

## 5. Tremble to forget it

'Take care lest you forget the Lord, who brought you out of the land of Egypt, out of the house of slavery.'                    v. 12

Moses interrupts his direct instruction with an aside in verse 10–12: he looks into the future, to days of prosperity. As well he might, because God has promised to prosper his people. But prosperity is dangerous.

Look around your church: you will probably see many prosperous families. There are a number of factors here and not all of them are a credit to the church. But one of them certainly is and it has been noted since the days of the Reformation and documented famously by the historian R. H. Tawney in his book 'Religion and the Rise of Capitalism'. The thesis is this: people who live by the Bible and love and trust the God of the Bible have a good work ethic. They also have a sensible and healthy lifestyle embracing moderation and eschewing excesses of all kinds. They are dutiful citizens; They value things like reading; they keep sensible hours and use their time well. Therefore they prosper in their business; their children do well at school and tend to avoid some of the pitfalls of youth. They in their turn grow up, advance in their careers, marry happily and faithfully and go on to raise happy and healthy children. A measure of prosperity often goes hand in hand with people who live God's way.

But prosperity is dangerous. It can make you self-satisfied and complacent because you are so very comfortable and have such a very pleasing way of life. That is when you take your eye off the ball, or, to revert to our original metaphor, it is when you drop the baton. You forget it was the Lord who has given you every good thing in your life and so all spiritual disciplines slowly slide into oblivion or into an increasingly meaningless appendage, just one among a number of lifestyle choices.

## 6. Target it

'It is the Lord your God you shall fear. Him you shall serve and by his name you shall swear. You shall not go after other gods, the gods of the peoples who are around you.'                                                    v. 13–14

'You shall do what is right and good in the sight of the Lord ...'
                                                                                            v. 18

Again in verses 13–19 Moses calls the parents back to living for God alone. Some Christian parents feel a tension between living for God and raising their children. They fear that to put God first (i.e. above their families) will somehow be to the detriment of their families.

But one of the greatest modern idolatries, is idolatry of the family. Hear the words of Jesus:

> 'whoever loves son or daughter more than me is not worthy of me.'
> Matthew 10:37

As we love and serve God, and as that love and service translates into love and service for others in our churches and communities for the gospel, our children have a chance to see the joy of living for something other than yourself. They need to see that at work. Don't rule it out for their sakes. Instead, bring them in.

## 7. Testify

> 'When your son asks you in time to come, "What is the meaning of the testimonies and the statutes and the rules that theLord our God has commanded you?" then you shall say to your son, "We were Pharaoh's slaves in Egypt. And the Lord brought us out ..."'
> VS 20–21

The daily, weekly, monthly and annual routines of our lives reflect our priorities. There is a reason why we do the things we do. The Israelites had their sacrifices and annual festivals which they observed carefully so that they would not forget what God had done for them and their own dependence on him.

So a Christian family will set up routines which will display the fact that Jesus is Lord. They will pray and read the Bible regularly; they will be part of a local church and faithfully attend its gatherings on Sundays and at other times. At particular times of year they may choose to particularly remember the incarnation of Jesus Christ or his death and resurrection. Whatever those routines are, make them meaningful and reasonable. Be prepared to explain what you do and why.

At the beginning of this chapter I pointed out that one of the differences between indoctrination and teaching is that teaching allows and invites questions and welcomes them as an opportunity to explain further. That is what is going on at the end of Deuteronomy 6, and elsewhere in the Pentateuch: when your son asks you … explain … 'we were Pharaoh's slaves in Egypt' …

This whole last section in verses 20–25 underlines the importance of personal testimony. We are not just passing on some useful ideas or a body of knowledge. We are talking about a God we know, a Saviour who loves us and died for us personally. The Israelites returned again and again to the story of their rescue from slavery. It is the archetypal story of the Old Testament and as such is a prefigurement of the greatest redemption story in the world. Our children will learn the story of Jesus' death and resurrection, but they also need to hear from you the story of how you came to know that 'the Son of God loved me and gave himself up for me' (Ephesians 5:2). In the end that is why you want to pass on this truth more than you want to pass on anything else. It is a transforming truth. God invades our lives and makes us new. He has done it for me and he can do it for you.

## Picking up the baton of truth

The very fact that the Bible calls upon parents to train and instruct their children—the words in Ephesians 6:4 could be equally translated discipline and admonition—reminds us again that our children are naturally wayward. They need God to open their blind eyes. They are dead in their sins until God raises them. So all your faithful teaching will not guarantee that they become Christians. God has children; he does not have grandchildren (John 1:12–13). Until your children receive Christ, believe in his name and thereby become his children, they are not saved, they are lost. They do not get into heaven on your ticket.

So is there no advantage to be born into a Christian home?

Of course there is: your child will hear the gospel. Your child will see the gospel lived out. Your child will be prayed for. To name but three.

And you have every reason to trust that as you pray for your children that God will make himself known to them, that he will answer and that the gospel will bear fruit in their lives. It may not be at the time you would like. Sometimes it is early, sometimes late. Your diligent teaching will ensure that they have all the right hooks in their mind so that one day when they hear the gospel (again) it will all make sense. Or they will respond regularly, trusting Christ increasingly in proportion to their growing understanding. God works in different ways. But he does work, by his Spirit, through his word.

## Some practical inferences and applications

There have already been many in this chapter but here are three more:

1. If you have become lax in your teaching of the children, take some time to understand why. Is it because you have too sentimental a view of children? Is it because of a sense of hypocrisy? Is it because your priorities have become inverted? Is it because of a feeling of inadequacy? All these are things that can be rectified through repentance and prayer.

2. If you consider (or your children are telling you) that your family Bible times are a bit samey and dull, investigate some new materials. Ask people at church what they do. Explore online for new ideas.

## For further reading/resources

'The Jesus Storybook Bible' by Sally Lloyd Jones

'The Big Picture Story Bible' by David Helm

'Ferdinand—the engine who went off the rails' by Ann Benton (Christian Focus)

Various Colin Buchanan CDs and DVDs. See www.colinbuchanan.com.au

# Chapter 12

# Can we trust our children to others?

## Home-schooling and its alternatives

*'I cannot imagine what information could be more terrifying than your hints and warnings,' exclaimed Frodo. 'I knew that danger lay ahead, of course; but I did not expect to meet it in our own Shire. Can't a hobbit walk from the water to the river in peace?'*

*'But it is not your own Shire,' said Gildor. 'Others dwelt here before hobbits were; and others will dwell here again when hobbits are no more. The wide world is all about you: you can fence yourselves in, but you cannot forever fence it out.'*

From 'The Fellowship of the Ring' by J.R.R.Tolkein

Universal, free education is a relatively recent idea in Britain, less than 150 years old. The 1870 Elementary Education Act made provision for the education of all children between 5 and 13. The 1880 Act made school compulsory; the 1891 Act made it free. Before the nineteenth century education was generally considered wasted on the poor; some even considered it dangerous. Only the children of the rich and the rising middle class went to school, and not all of those, since many were educated by tutors at home.

It was evangelical Christians who first started educating the masses. The original Sunday schools were very much about literacy. These big-hearted believers wanted people to be able to access the Bible. Other philanthropists caught on and managed to persuade the state that an educated lower class would make a better workforce than an uneducated one.

We tend to associate education with going to school. But education is first and foremost the business of the parent. A child learns more in his first five years than he does in the rest of his life. A child's brain is wired to learn. Before he meets a teacher in a professional capacity a child will have learnt a language, maybe more than one, some mathematics, IT, music, art, literature, geography, history and science. Of course there is passive learning and there is active learning and those who are encouraged in the latter will make more progress but they will all learn something. Similarly there is passive teaching, by default, and there is active teaching. But in every case, for better or worse, a child's primary teachers are his parents.

## The choice

By the time a child's fifth birthday comes around, his parents will have made a conscious or unconscious choice: to delegate a large part of their child's future education to others, or to do it themselves. This latter option is entirely legal and there is surprisingly minimal state interference. Many parents automatically take the delegation option which means sending their children either to a state school or to an independent fee-paying one. Some parents start their children in school but at a later stage opt out and take on the business of home education. In most cases it would be mothers who shoulder the burden of the actual teaching.

It does us, as parents, no harm to think about the choice we make in this regard and the reasons for making it. Can we trust our children to others? Should we? In the light of the increasingly secular ethos of twenty-first century Britain and of the kind of issues I have raised in this book, perhaps Christian parents should gather their children into their castles and raise the drawbridge.

People home-school for a variety of reasons. Some do it because they can and because they want to; others do it because they dislike the local state provision or because geographically it is difficult to access a suitable school. Many overseas missionaries are in that category. There are also those who home-school because of the special needs of their children.

Some home educators, however, are on the offensive. They maintain that to send their children to a state school would be to hand them over to Satan. Such parents have a missionary zeal about their choice which can be somewhat alarming.

## The argument for home-schooling

### 1. A question of conscience

The Christian couple I spoke to at length had not started out as home educators. They accepted that they had no way of seeing the whole picture of what went on at their children's local primary school but the things they heard bothered them. A big issue was the pluralistic aspect of the assemblies. A Muslim teacher told the children that she worshipped the same God as the Christians did; at Easter time when the children were asked why Jesus died, they were told that all their answers were correct, when they clearly were not; there was a trip to a Hindu temple where all the children received a Hindu blessing. The parents considered this was extremely confusing to a growing child.

They were also worried about the secularisation of the curriculum. It put God in a box and made him increasingly irrelevant. These two aspects in particular troubled their consciences and made them wonder if they were doing the right thing by their children. They talked to some other home educators and liked what they heard. They found it an exciting and very attractive idea, although they were well aware it was beyond their means. Home schooling requires that the family can manage financially on one income. At that time this was not practical. But they prayed about it.

God answered their prayers unexpectedly by a new job opportunity for the husband and father which meant better paid work nearer home. The couple felt that this was God's confirmation that they should de-register their children from school and begin to educate at home.

## 2. God in every lesson

They spoke of the huge blessing that decision was bringing them. They relished the extended contact with their children. Previously they had been giving the best six hours of every weekday of their children's lives to others; now the mother enjoyed knowing her children better.

They loved the fact that now every part of the curriculum included God. He is the God who orders history as well as the Creator behind every scientific law. They had worked hard to research the curriculum and the resource options. Mostly they had bought in textbooks but the mother had enjoyed setting her own history curriculum and following the children's interests.

Home-schooling is very time-efficient. Because there was no time wasted on assemblies, administration and travel, lessons at home were done in four mornings of the week. At other times the children were taken to meet up with other home-schoolers for swimming and skating lessons. The teaching of languages and some musical instrumental tuition were outsourced. There was plenty of time left in the day for play and the siblings had developed a strong bond. When lessons were over they were very good at entertaining themselves. They had made a wide range of friendships through the home-schooling network.

## 3. Character training

Another big plus was the way in which these parents believed their children's characters were developing. Through home education they had been taught a strong work ethic and loved learning. In fact they saw the whole of life as learning and did not place an artificial division between lessons and life. They were also protected from the tackier side of school (like, for example, school discos); they were free to enjoy being children and to grow up at their own pace.

The parents found the whole thing much less stressful than being a slave to the timings and whims of school. There were no demands to suddenly produce, for example, a Saxon costume; there was no pressure to find the money for an overpriced school residential. There was the liberty and flexibility of being able to design their own programme, space out the breaks and take holidays when they chose. The parents felt in control and were extremely positive.

## The argument against home-schooling

### 1. The expertise of others

Despite the undoubted sincerity and enthusiasm of home educators, not everyone would be convinced that they could do a better job than a school. For a start, some parents could not manage the family budget on just one full-time wage neither could they afford the cost of resources. And some would doubt whether they had the skills. Just because you enjoy home-made chutney, you might not want to make it yourself. The process makes the house stink of garlic, onions and vinegar; it might make sense to just buy it at the supermarket.

Or suppose you have a problem with an appliance. You can mend it yourself or you can call for an engineer. The thing is—some of us know that if we tried to mend it ourselves we would probably make things worse. It's a no-brainer, we say. Send for the expert and be thankful.

When it comes to schooling their children, there are those who have neither the leisure nor the ability to do it themselves. And some do not have the inclination. They are happy to send their children to school, and not merely as a default option. As a trained and experienced primary school teacher, I myself could have home-schooled my children. But my husband and I decided to send them to the local state primary school.

## 2. Odd enough

Swimming against the tide is no new thing for Christians. There are plenty of ways, including those highlighted in this book, in which Christians always have been a peculiar people. There are plenty of ways in which to live Biblically you have to be different. Children of faith families are an oddity. Perhaps especially children of those in Christian ministry are odd. We considered our children were odd enough. Let them at least go to school along with the other children in our street.

We were also concerned about the message that home education would give to our neighbours. We hoped to share Christ with them but we feared they would read our refusal to send our children to the school their children attended as a statement of rejection, as though their children were not good enough to associate with ours. We thought this would be counter-productive to our attempts to be salt and light in our communities.

We appreciated the interface that standing at the school gate gave with other local parents. People are all too ready to suspect Christians and dismiss Christianity. We found that rubbing shoulders with other parents gave us opportunity to express what we had in common and led to opportunities for serving the community and witnessing for Christ which we would not otherwise have had. We had in mind the teaching of 1 Peter 2.

> 'Beloved, I urge you as sojourners and exiles to abstain from the passions of the flesh, which wage war against your soul. Keep your conduct *among the Gentiles* honourable, so that when they speak against you as evildoers, they may see your good deeds and glorify God on the day of visitation.'          1 Peter 2:11–12 (Emphasis mine)

We believed that living among the Gentiles, or 'pagans' (as other versions have it) included sending our children to the local school. That Scripture reminds us that what wars against the soul is not the pagan neighbours, but the sinful desires within. The real enemy is, and always has been, indwelling sin.

### 3. Home wins

As a schoolteacher I had been all too aware of the overriding influence of home. Sometimes for the good of a child I wished the school *could* outweigh a very negative home background. The difference a teacher can make is very small. That is the sad truth. But it is a cheering truth for a Christian parent. What you do at home counts for more—your teaching, example and attitude are what will colour your child's thinking and character with a deeper dye than anything the school can come up with.

Even quite young children spot the difference. And as they meet ideas at variance with what their parents believe they may come home with questions, which just present you the parent with further opportunities to teach. They would have to meet these ideas sometime and we considered that from the earliest age our children should understand not only what we believed but why we believed it. This constituted part of their training in discernment. So we did not see other faiths and worldviews as a threat. In some ways it just enabled the gospel light to shine more clearly.

Daniel 1 gives an example of some young people thrust into an alien culture. True, they were not five or six years old but they were school age and their removal from Jerusalem to Babylon was an extreme separation. They were not going home to tea with Mum and Dad every night. At Babylon High their minds were saturated in Babylonian lore and literature which would have included a serious amount of idolatrous claptrap. Even their names were changed. But they still remained true to their early training. They still were able to draw the line. That is what they did when they refused to eat the king's food. They were making a statement. They had not forgotten who the real king is. They were clear about who writes history and who calls the shots. Home wins.

## 4. Common grace

The doctrine of common grace says that God has generously held back from the planet the worst ravages of the fall. So Christians do not have the monopoly on kindness, decency, and serviceable gifts. The world is full of delightful people who have all sorts of talents and abilities and many of those people are found in the teaching profession. By God's common grace our children were taught by some excellent teachers, who were not believers but had useful skills and inspiring knowledge to impart. They were generous and warm and worked hard to help our children learn. Of course there were the duff ones as well—all schools have some of those—but our children coped. We were happy for them to be part of the general melee. Yes there is a ridiculous amount of time wasted in the school day. But we thought it quite healthy for our children to learn to have put up with not everything being tailor-made for their personal needs. There was opportunity within that setting for them to take responsibility for their own learning and behaviour. They had to make choices and face consequences.

As chairman of governors of a local school for a dozen years, I sat on many interview panels. I was always very glad when I could appoint a Christian teacher. But experience taught me that the Christians I appointed were not necessarily the best teachers. They were generally lovely colleagues and hard-working members of staff, who did their very best and were faithful witnesses in the school, but faith in Jesus Christ does not automatically make you a brilliant teacher.

## Everything has its downside

The home-schoolers I spoke to accepted that they couldn't replicate everything that was done at school e.g. team sports or school productions. But they considered that these needs could be met in other ways. Their eldest daughter, aged 11, had commented that she would have liked going off to (secondary) school on her own. The parents recognised this as a need to exercise some independence and were attempting to build in some opportunities in that regard. They said there were sacrifices involved in terms of money and commitment. Resources cost money and the family now had to manage on one income. Their lifestyle had changed: the mother rarely if ever had the house to herself, although she said that was not the problem she had at first thought it might be.

Another Christian couple I spoke to had made the opposite shift. They had tried home-schooling for a year and then put their children into school. The father spoke of his relief. He said about the previous year, 'I lost my wife: a teacher moved in instead and the whole house was a classroom.' They also had concerns about the all-consuming nature of home education, which meant that serving in the church took very much second place.

But there are problems within the state school curriculum. A big one is PSHE (personal, social and health education) and citizenship. Much of this is wishy-washy nonsense but potentially in the light of recent legislation it can be pernicious. Thankfully many sensible teachers do not take it very seriously and it often gets side-lined. But it is a slot for pressure-group propaganda of all sorts. It is a space to be watched.

No less a problem is the recent official outlawing of the teaching of intelligent design in the science curriculum. These are issues which require careful handling and there is an urgent need for churches to take responsibility for some clarity of Biblical instruction on these subjects. And I am not here just referring to the needs of schoolchildren.

With these kinds of problems in mind, Christians in some places have got together and organised their own schools, under a variety of different auspices and funding and admissions arrangements. These schools have more liberty, curriculum-wise, to be Biblical and God-centred. They may also have some of the disadvantages of home-schooling. But where such schools exist they present another alternative for a parent to consider. They are too diverse for me to discuss here.

## The limits of education

Whether your children are educated at home or at school, every parent needs to recognise what a school cannot do. It cannot give a new heart. There are no guarantees for the end-products of any kind of education that they will follow Christ. There is no place for smug self-satisfaction in any of us.

There is also no place for judgmentalism. A pastor told me that education was a subject he had learned to keep away from because it engendered such high feeling and division in the church family. Many parents were either militant or defensive. Parents should be careful not to make their own choice in this regard a standard by which they judge others. Every Christian must act according to conscience in this area. Let us respect the decisions of others and all seek to raise our children to the glory of God.

As this century progresses there may increasingly be more pressing reasons for Christians to consider the home-school option or the Christian school. We can be grateful to live in a country where these choices are still available. That may not always be the case. Who knows?

In the meantime parents seek to behave responsibly as those who must give an account. Whatever choice we make as parents in regard to education, ultimately we entrust our children to God and seek his protection and blessing on their lives.

If we are wise, we will all, sooner or later, attempt to train our children to think through the challenges of a prevailing culture which is hostile to Christians. The question is whether you can do that better by fencing your children in or by letting them out there to face it.

What is clear is that, as Gildor said to Frodo, 'The wide world is all about you: you can fence yourselves in, but you cannot forever fence it out.'

## Some practical inferences and applications:

1. Whether you have chosen to outsource education or do it yourself, how will you prepare your child to stand in a hostile culture?

2. Is there a positive way you could have some input into your child's school? *'A man's gift makes room for him and brings him before the great.'* (Proverbs 18:16) You may have something to give which will not only open the way to witness for Christ but also to make your feedback, even where negative, more readily received. There are formal opportunities such as being a governor or part of the fund-raising team. But there also many informal ways of getting involved through music, reading with children or running an after-school club. Perhaps you can start or join a parents' prayer group and meet with others to pray for the school. This mirrors God's instruction to the Israelites exiled in Babylon: *'But seek the welfare of the city where I have sent you into exile, and pray to the Lord on its behalf, for in its welfare you will find your welfare'* (Jeremiah 29:7).

# Chapter 13

# Sunday blessings or Sunday blues

## Children and church

*Six months previously a young minister of the Wesleyan Circuit, to whom heaven had denied both a sense of humour and a sense of honour, had committed the infamy of starting a Bible class for big boys on a Saturday afternoons. This outrage had appalled and disgusted the boyhood of Wesleyanism in Bursley. Their afternoon for games, their only fair afternoon in the desert of the week, to be filched from them and used against them for such an odious purpose as a Bible class! Not only Sunday school on a Sunday afternoon, but a Bible class on Saturday afternoon! It was incredible. It was unbearable. It was gross tyranny, and nothing else. Nevertheless the young minister had his way, by dint of meanly calling upon parents and invoking their help.*

*The scurvy worm actually got together a class of twelve to fifteen boys, to the end of securing their eternal welfare. And they had to attend the class, though they swore they never would, and they had to sing hymns, and they had to kneel and listen to prayers, and they had to listen to the most intolerable tedium; and to take notes of it. All this while the sun was shining, or the rain was raining, on fields and streets and open spaces and ponds!*

From 'Clayhanger' by Arnold Bennett

I must state straight away that I will not be making the case for a Saturday afternoon Bible class. I quote Arnold Bennett to show that the idea that church is a cruel imposition on children is not new: 'Clayhanger' was published in 1910. Over a century later a Christian roadshow for parents and youth leaders entitled 'Getting your children through church without them ending up hating God' shows that the assumption/expectation that church is a turn-off is as live and kicking as the children we Christian parents apparently treat so meanly.

There are statistics to back up this idea. According to Christian Research, churches in the UK will have lost an estimated 1.1 million children between 1990 and 2020. Projections in keeping with present trends suggest that in 2020 183,700 will attend church, compared with 375,300 in 2010.

You don't have to be a statistician to want to unpack those figures a bit more. What do they mean by children? What do they mean by church? Are these children offspring of believers or those who are dropped off at church activities by non-Christian parents? But whatever the answer to those pertinent questions, few of us can doubt that there is certainly leakage of young people from the gathered church. Most of us will be acquainted with middle-aged Christians who grieve over the spiritual waywardness of their offspring. Some of those blame the church: it was too strict and their children were not welcome; it was too child-centred and the transition to ordinary services was a gap to wide to be bridged.

## What shall we do about church?

In view of all the negative press the church gets, Christian parents might almost feel obliged to apologise to their children for taking them to a service or as some would put it 'making them go'. How dare we take them to something so intrinsically tedious? We wouldn't put it like that, quite, but we might do all sorts of things to soften what we are being taught to see as 'a blow'. So we might be inclined to:

Get it over as quickly and briefly as possible so that there is plenty of time left on Sunday for 'fun'

Hang loose to church events and programmes

Go along with a whole bag of sweeteners, which might include literal sweets, but also myriad distractions and diversions to see the child through.

Limit our expectations of attendance and attention to the bare minimum

I hope you spotted some of the lies and false assumptions there, but let us spell some of them out.

## Lies we believe

1. 'Anything a child is "made to do" is going to be counter-productive.' On the contrary. Do we take that view of bedtime or meals or clothing or school? No. Parents decide what is best from day 1. All parents impose things on their children; it is a right use of loving authority, based on the premise that children are not in a position to make wise choices for themselves. Of course the old mantra 'rules without relationship lead to rebellion' is as true about church as it is about anything. Your training of children in any area will only be effective in the context of a warm relationship.

2. Children cannot be expected to sit still and listen. Wrong. If you expect your children to not be able to do something they almost certainly won't. In fact the more toys and diversions you bring along to church, the less they will be inclined to sit still because they will get the underlying message that they would not, could not, just sit in a pew and watch and listen. Actually, children often meet expectations when they are clearly and positively expressed and when they have support and good role-modelling. Of course some children are more fidgety than others and you may need to enforce your expectations rigorously and forcefully. But children can be trained and children can learn. And this is good general discipline.

3. Everything should be child-centred. Or, to put it another way, it is a crime against childhood to bore a child. Wrong again. It is extremely unhealthy for a child to grow up thinking that everything in life must be organised for their entertainment. I am not arguing that the presence of children should be ignored in times of public worship. There is a place for directly

addressing the young as the Bible does in much of Proverbs and in numerous epistles. (Colossians 3:20; 1 John 2:12; 1 Peter 5:6). There is a place for age-appropriate instruction since as Paul acknowledges in 1 Corinthians 13:11 those who are children think like children, which is different from adult thinking. But not all the time. In fact one of the points of church is to restate on a weekly basis that God is the centre, not us.

4. Sunday is a family day. While it is true that hard-working families enjoy the fact that on Sunday they have more time to spend together, Sunday is primarily the Lord's day (Revelation 1:10). He ordained the one day in seven so that we feeble and forgetful human-beings should remember to honour him who created us, provides for us and redeemed us. Not that there need be tension between keeping the Lord's day and family life, as I hope this chapter will show. But if there is, we do our children no favours when we give the message that their needs and happiness are always paramount.

5. Church can never be fun. Fun might not be quite the right word but there is every indication in the Bible that worship is to be glad and joyful. If we adults have made it miserable and wearisome then shame on us.

> 'You shall rejoice in your feast, you and your son and your daughter, your male servant and your female servant, the Levite, the sojourner, the fatherless, and the widow who are within your towns.'
>
> Deuteronomy 16:14

If your idea of fun is ease, self-indulgence, excess, vulgarity or brash behaviour, then certainly don't look for it in a church. But if your children can find pleasure in the company of delightful human beings; happy interaction with a wide range of people; heart-warming, uplifting music; opportunities for engaging body, mind and spirit in worship and in service; they can have fun at church. Most important of all, if they have not yet learned to rejoice in the Lord themselves, they can witness others doing just that.

## Two theological reasons to go to church

### 1. We owe God worship

To worship God is to give him only what is his due. We are not doing God a favour when we turn up at church and give him a couple of hours of our time. As Psalm 100 puts it, after the general injunction to all the earth to worship the Lord with gladness and come before him with joyful songs, it is God who made us; we did not make ourselves. To refuse to offer God our worship is treason. He does not owe us; we owe him. This worship is due to him from all classes of society and all ages of people (not to mention all living things and even the weather):

'... Kings of the earth and all peoples,
princes and all rulers of the earth!
Young men and maidens together,
old men and children!

Let them praise the name of the Lord,
for his name alone is exalted;
his majesty is above earth and heaven;'          Psalm 148:11–13

Knowing we are liable to get distracted and forget, God

enshrined one day in the week when people would routinely cease from the activities of the other six, except as is in keeping with necessity or mercy, and focus on him. This is given not as a burden, but as a rest—a foretaste of heaven and a generous kindness and wise balance to our busy lives. What a relief, for one day to put our cares and labours aside and delight in our Maker and all he has done for us. This is an aspect of Sunday which children can be taught to appreciate—the things that are not required of us because it is Sunday. We did not allow our children to do their homework on a Sunday—that is one way of putting it. Our preferred way was to say that on Sunday we allowed them to not do their homework. There were happier and better things to do. This is liberty, not bondage! You do not have to be a strict Sabbatarian to see what a healthy antidote this is to workaholism, and also what a delightful break from consumerism and materialism. It is a boon to any parent to instil at an early age limits to certain activities, whether TV, computers, phone-using, schoolwork, football, partying etc. The wisdom of the fourth commandment enables a parent to say benignly and legitimately 'Give it a rest'.

## 2. Church is one of God's big ideas

The church is a key part of God's redemption plan, not a lifestyle-choice supplement. The apostle Paul gets very excited about the church in his letter to the Ephesians. For example, in chapter 3 when he writes about God's intention in salvation, the climax is that people are brought together through the gospel to be 'members of one body' (v. 6). The church has significance even beyond this earth. The church, i.e. the redeemed people of God as a unit, is to make a statement to the cosmos, 'the rulers and authorities in the heavenly realms', about the wisdom of God in his eternal redemptive purposes. A Christian can never therefore have a low or negligent attitude to the church. Every Christian is a member of the body and that membership should be expressed by membership of a local church. This is central to a believer's life and growth. Christian parents will want to introduce their children to church at the earliest age because of the importance of the church in their own lives.

## Three practical reasons to go to church

### 1. A pool of support

There is an African proverb to the effect that it takes a village to raise a child. In other words children thrive when they are part of a community. The local church provides a community much more cohesive and benign than the average village. It is a community bound together by the love of Christ expressed in the gospel. Within that community is a pool of support, experience and wisdom to support the young parent. There will be a range of excellent role models for children and there are people who will pray doggedly for their salvation. At a very practical level we discovered that we could clothe our children for their first ten years almost entirely from hand-me-downs from the church family, not to mention toys and equipment. It takes a church to raise a child.

Our own children benefited enormously from this wide and varied community. There were those there who took trouble to get to know them as individuals, those who invited them out (without their parents), sent them parcels of goodies when they went off to university and those who read the Bible with them and shared not only the gospel but their lives. What not to like?

## 2. A positive peer group

Many parents fear and dread the effect of peer group pressure on their children. But I would like to point out that it all depends on the peer group. None of us is impervious to the opinions of our peers and sometimes this can be a positive motivational factor, not a million miles from accountability. A wholesome peer group at your local church might keep your children on the right lines even before they have trusted Christ. But while they hang in and turn up for the sake of their friends they are still hearing the gospel. Furthermore they will be doing innocuous things like playing table-tennis, which is not an activity to cause the average parent many sleepless nights.

A Sunday school is not just about teaching children the Bible, although that might be its stated aim. It is also about providing a safe haven for children of believers. In twentieth-century Britain children from Christian families can be considered very strange, but at church they can comfortably mingle with others whose parents are odd like theirs. Friendships made in such a context generally prove to be in the long run more vital and fruitful than those made with classmates at school.

## 3. Different voice, same message

Although the passing on of the baton truth is the job first and foremost of a Christian parent, it does no harm at all for a child to hear the same message from a range of other people and in a variety of settings. Familiarity can sometimes breed contempt or harden a resistant heart. So a different voice may sometimes get more readily through the defences because of its alternative approach or style. This is a role for the youth activities at church. It is also the reason why camps, holiday clubs and youth conferences are often times of reaping the harvest of fields patiently sown over many years by a faithful parent.

## What can children gain from a church service?

### 1. They witness worship

I cannot find in Scripture anything to suggest that one can catch a new heart just by sitting next to a worshipper, nor that words which are beyond the comprehension of an infant are likely to edify. After all wasn't that why Paul insisted on interpretation of tongues (1 Corinthians 14)? Just hearing all that very spiritual but incomprehensible talk was not going to profit anybody. Because of this I personally am in favour of children leaving the gathering at some point for a crèche or some age-appropriate instruction. But there are very good reasons for having the children in with their parents for at least part of the time: they need to witness God's people declaring his praises; they need to know that not everything in this life is for their personal entertainment; they need to learn to value God's church as a unity of people of all ages and types. They won't learn those things if they are always segregated and provided with a bespoke service.

### 2. They can learn to worship

I salute the parents who bring their children into the service without props and aids and expect and encourage their children to participate as much as they are able in the service going on around them.

I recognise of course that worship is a heart activity and you have no control of your children's hearts. But you can train them in attitudes and habits which make worship possible, achievable and even joyful, instead of giving the impression that worship is for the grown-ups and they can do what they like as long as they don't embarrass you in front of the congregation. I am sad that when I speak on parenting to various Christian groupings I am often asked the question, 'At what age should our children be allowed to opt out of church?'

## Church without tears

### 1. Expectation

Again, so much is about expectation. Where you see teenagers continue to happily attend church, twice on Sunday, along with their parents, it will be firstly because their parents have cheerfully built this unquestioned routine into their lives since birth. It is what they do on Sunday. It defines them as a family and they do it gladly. They would no more opt out of church than they would opt out of eating.

### 2. Attitude

Another observation about families who do church without tears is that they are wholly positive about church, which they see as not just important, but good. These are the families where the parents take time off work to be involved in Holiday Bible Club; one of them will unfailingly be at the prayer meeting; they will frequently be offering hospitality and doing works of mercy. Interestingly, in my experience it tends to be the offspring of those who attend more sparingly, sometimes on grounds of being with the family, who see their family walk away from church. That is a generalisation but it is an observable trend.

## 3. Saturday night and Sunday morning

Sometimes our Sundays would go much better if we gave them some forethought. The family who arrive during the first hymn, having had battles over clothing and downed breakfast against the clock, are already hassled before they take their seats. They are not ready to worship and certainly not ready to help their children to do the same.

In our house Sunday began on Saturday evening. Knowing the challenge of getting everybody washed, dressed, breakfasted and out of the house on time, I used some of Saturday evening for things which would make Sundays calmer and more cheerful. I would prepare as much of Sunday dinner as was practicable the day before. This left me free to attend to the children. I would also decide on Saturday, with their cooperation when old enough, what they would be wearing and it would be all laid out for the morning before they went to bed.

Sunday breakfast was not much later than weekday breakfast but they all had to be there. And they wanted to be because it was the best one of the week. My husband always cooked Sunday breakfast. Being a pastor he always left soon afterwards and went to church ahead of us, so I escorted our four by myself.

## 4. Make Sunday special

Breakfast was just one of the ways in which we signalled to our children that Sunday was a great day and a different one. The Israelites were encouraged to celebrate God by feasts and Sunday dinner in our house was also always a comparative feast. It was the only dinner of the week where there was a proper pudding—

sometimes more than one—and there was usually a fairly decent joint of meat.

Church was good because of the people and we often invited others to join us for lunch. Our children either entertained our guests in the sitting room or assisted me in the kitchen. We had Sunday music, Sunday stories, Sunday games and Sunday sweets. I do not record this to boast about our own family life as if it was hassle free, nor do I intend to imply that the routines, prohibitions and sideshows we used to signify the preciousness and specialness of Sunday are a pattern for others to follow. We had our issues and moods like any family, but we did not give up on Sundays. Every family is capable of making Sunday special in their own way but in a way which builds around the immovable fixture of church a many-layered experience which is glad, warm, inclusive and God-honouring.

## 5. Pew tactics

Again, the following comments are mere suggestions but I would reiterate the point that unless you are explicit about what you are coming to church for and what you expect of your children, the time spent in the service, however long or short, will be sheer endurance. So here follows a list of ideas you might dare to try, as appropriate:

- Arrive in good time and let your child enjoy a bit of meeting and greeting

- Sit near the front of the church—much less distracting

- Sit with your children, or insist they sit with you, until you are absolutely convinced that they will be committed to engaging in the worship, unmoved by the antics of their peers. It may not be cool but encourage them that there will be time afterwards to hang out with their friends.

- Allow no props, toys or other irrelevant items. Instead be cheerfully single-minded about focussing on God, our maker and offering him the worship due to his name.

- Once the service begins, signal that you expect the children to pay attention and sit facing the front either on their own seat or on your lap. Gentle prods, nudges and frowns will discourage fidgets; warm cuddles and smiles will encourage compliance. Whisper words of explanation and encouragement.

- Model enthusiastic participation. Sing out in the hymns, bow your head in prayer, say 'Amen', open your Bible and look up every reference.

- If the church uses a hymn book, point to the words as they are sung, even for non-readers. Young children find it difficult to follow words from a screen so if this is the system, get hold of a words-sheet which is usually provided for those with sight issues.

- Allow small children to stand on the seat to participate in the singing. Encourage the making of a joyful noise.

- Set up a habit where the pre-literate child squeezes your hand every time a certain keyword appears in the hymn or prayer or reading.

Of course there will be bad days and sometimes you might meet noisy resistance, which will cause you to flee red-faced from the sanctuary with a writhing child in your arms. Use the time out to explain calmly once again why it is important to honour God, whom we can't see, but who sees us and knows us all the time. Talk through what kind of behaviour you expect to see next time.

## Promoted to evening service

For our children it was a privilege and an honour to be allowed to attend evening service. When they were small it was only done on high days and holidays and they discovered that this was what the cool, older young people at church did. So once they had shown that they could sit still and listen to a sermon, perhaps taking notes as an aid to concentration we allowed them to go regularly. It was a rite of passage and they were very happy to be part of this meeting of the church which had a more adult flavour than the morning family service.

We were well aware that their motivation for going was frequently social rather than spiritual. And we said nothing, being aware that they were unfinished business as far as God was concerned. Their confession of faith, when it happened, was all the more precious and certainly worth waiting for.

## The pilgrim family

We know it is God who saves. We cannot make our children Christians by 'making' them come to church. Parents cannot induce conversion, nor should they try. But to bring them to church and expect their compliance with this family routine as long as they live under the same roof as minors is not unreasonable. With the loving authority delegated to us by God we can state our intentions as Joshua did, 'As for me and my house, we will serve the Lord' (Joshua 24:15). Counter-cultural it certainly is, but consider what else they might be doing and be unembarrassed and unflinching.

It did not occur to me all those years I hustled our four out of the house and up the road to church that this peculiar routine was being observed by our neighbours. But it came out later in casual conversation, often with grudging admiration: 'How on earth did you get your teenagers up on a Sunday morning?'

It really wasn't that hard.

## Some practical inferences and applications

1. Jesus said, 'Let the little children come to me and do not hinder them.' In what ways do we hinder children from coming to Jesus?

2. *'Fear of man lays a snare,'* (Proverbs 29:25). Many Christian parents find themselves pre-eminently aware at church of what others think about their way of handling the children. This can cause them to be either over-strict or loath to correct, depending on who is watching. What is the answer to this problem? Read the next chapter.

## For further reading
'Parenting in the Pew' by Robbie Castleman (IVP books)

# Chapter 14

# Aims and ambitions

## What do we want for our children?

*There was a young man from Darjeeling,*
*Who travelled from London to Ealing.*
*It said on the door,*
*'Please don't spit on the floor',*
*So he carefully spat on the ceiling.*

It is comparatively easy to identify the things you don't like. In the writing of this book I have tried to draw to the attention of Christian parents some aspects of contemporary culture which are at odds with a Biblical worldview. Readers may recognise in these issues some pitfalls to avoid. But like the man from Darjeeling it is possible to do things differently without those things being necessarily better.

So a reader might work hard to be clear about the moral framework; he might be unafraid to correct and diligent to instruct. He might be impressively non-materialistic and enjoy a fantastic relationship with his children. And he might be carefully spitting on the ceiling.

## Parental ambitions

When I run my parenting course there is a session in which I ask those present to imagine their children grown up. 'Write a list of adjectives,' I say, 'to describe the person you would like your child to become.'

Mostly what people write down is a list of Christian virtues, which then gives me the opportunity to open up the discussion into the realm of values, where we get them, why we love them and how we instil them. Even non-Christians never include in their lists words like rich, famous or beautiful. They know that ultimately these things have little value or importance.

But Christians nearly always put at the top of that list that they want their children to believe the gospel and follow Jesus Christ. Many Christian parents would say that ambition was the only one that really mattered. They might echo the words of the apostle John when he writes:

'I have no greater joy than to hear that my children are walking in the truth.' 3 John 4

Now if we have read our Bibles we know that doesn't happen by genetics or by contagion. You have to be born again. This book has explored some of the ways in which parents can teach and model and pray to that end.

But why do we want our children to be Christians?

## Five secondary (and rather lightweight) reasons to aim for godliness

- We want our children to be like us. We want a united family, who share common goals and values.

- We want our children to be happy. And we know that living God's way is the happiest way to live.

- We want our children to be good. It is so pleasant to be around well-behaved, decent, moral people.

- We want our children to be nice. The world is short on love and kindness and all those other virtues which are part of the Christian package.

- We want our children to be spiritual. It is such a refreshingly alternative way to live, when everyone else is so materialistic. It is excellent to train a child to appreciate things that money can't buy. Let them remember there is a God in heaven.

Now, each of the above is true and we may be honest enough to admit to thinking those things at times. But as motivation all they add up to is lifestyle choice. So let us play devil's advocate for a moment.

## Five arguments for secular child-rearing

- It is excitingly modern. Christianity is frankly out of date and out of touch. Modern people have science—they do not need God.

- It is extremely liberating. Christianity and its rules is a straitjacket. We can work out for ourselves the way we wish to direct our children.

- It is wonderfully easy. You don't have to keep getting anxious about what is right and wrong. Just do what you want.

- It is immensely popular. All your friends are doing it. You can keep in with the 'in' crowd and go with the flow.

- It is (generally) legal. Whereas Christianity can get you into trouble, if you stick your neck out.

Believers will spot at least the more obvious lies in the above; others will be uncovered in this chapter. But the lies and half-truths can be seductive. It can be hard to go against the tide all the time. We need to really know why we are doing it. To be a Christian is to be out of step of the world. To live by the Bible is unfashionable. It can make you unpopular. In some parts of the world it is illegal and can even get you put in prison.

Think carefully. Do you really want that for your children?

So what are we missing? What are we forgetting?

## The forgotten dimension

After all, there are plenty of atheists who prosper and whose children are well-mannered, charming and sensible.

That was precisely the position of Asaph, the writer of Psalm 73. His faith suffered a serious wobble when he observed how unbelievers thrive.

'they have no pangs until death ...'                                    v.4

'they are not stricken like the rest of mankind ...'                    v.5

'... always at ease, they increase in riches.'                         v.12

If Asaph had been raising children at that point, he might have argued for a secular approach. Why go against the tide? It's a waste of time and extremely hard work (v. 13 & 14).

Later on Asaph was really glad he didn't speak out and persuade others to abandon the life of faith in God. To do so would have been to betray God's children (v. 15). Not because his observations about the prosperity of the wicked were erroneous, but because his snapshot of them was static, not dynamic. It was a close-up, not the long view. It was totally misleading.

Asaph needed a wide-angle lens and he found it 'in the sanctuary of God' (v. 17). That is where he remembered what he had been forgetting, what we all so easily forget. The sanctuary of God is the place of the word of God and prayer. This is another reminder that we need to apply ourselves to those as a daily necessity and never ever neglect them, lest we betray our own children with a limited and therefore false perspective.

## What Asaph learned in the sanctuary

'... I went into the sanctuary of God; then I discerned their end.'

Psalm 73:17

### 1. An eternal perspective

In his excellent book '*Forever*', Paul David Tripp writes about how easy it is for Christians to live as eternity amnesiacs. Everybody around us is living for the here and now. All they hold precious is here. They want to fulfil their dreams in this life. And even our very sound training of our children can shift focus to the here and now, leading them to be satisfied with a good life on this earth. But as Tripp says, 'Life has a plot and the plot moves all of us to a destiny.'

As G. K. Chesterton said, 'You never met a mortal soul in your life.' When your child was born, an immortal soul came into the world. We muse and daydream about what our children will be and we want the best for them. But the best in life is worthless if they are not rich toward God. (Luke 12:21). We might encourage our children to compete for the best prizes. The apostle Paul uses similar language: 'Do you not know that in a race all the runners run, but only one receives the prize? So run that you may obtain it,' he says (1 Corinthians 9:24). But he is talking about a crown that will last for ever. This life's laurels wilt and fade and are forgotten. Walk round a graveyard. Your children's bodies, just as yours, will, unless Jesus returns first, certainly come to dust. But that is not the end of the story.

In the sanctuary Asaph is reminded that destruction awaits all who ignore God (v. 27). If the train is heading over the cliff, those who travel first class will not escape. Prosperity in this life is short and uncertain; destruction is certain, sudden and very great. Everything is about destination.

That is why we want our children to follow Jesus: because, in his words, 'the gate is wide and the way is easy that leads to destruction, and those who enter by it are many. For the gate is narrow and the way is hard that leads to life, and those who find it are few' (Matthew 7:13–14).

Imagine taking your child to the station. You are to put him on the train to Haslemere where he will be met by his grandparents to visit them there. But due to some confusion you actually put him on the train to Reading instead. The train leaves the station and you cheerfully wave him goodbye and then you realise your mistake. But he is already on that train now and he can't get off. That is the kind of thing a parent might have nightmares about. It serves as a chilling illustration to remind parents of ultimate destinations.

## 2. An understanding of consequences

Asaph learns that you reap what you sow. God is not mocked (Galatians 6:7). Everything comes to harvest. Life moves forward and the choices we make put us onto a particular road. It is not random, in this world or the next. Nor is it impersonal. God has his hands on the controls (Psalm 73:18). An understanding of consequences can be used in someone's life to bring them to fear their eternal destiny and seek a new start from the most gracious

God. Difficulties in this life, many of which we bring on ourselves, are at most temporary. They are not forever. Heaven is forever.

### 3. A place for grace

Asaph has made a serious error in his reckoning. He describes himself as senseless and ignorant, 'a brute beast'. That is the first effect perhaps of spending some time in the sanctuary. It is humbling to recognise how very stupid we are by nature, but that is the place to start. Atheism is sheer unadulterated folly as well as treason.

But then Asaph is bowled over by the fact that God still loves him. Instead of walking off in disgust at Asaph's foolish attitude, God sticks with him, takes him by the hand and leads him to the alternative destination—glory (verses 23–24). This is sheer, unadulterated grace.

We are all on the wrong train by nature, heading for a place we would not want to be. But in the life of a Christian, God has graciously stopped the train and opened the door to let us out. God is the one who rescues and redeems and brings us into the kingdom of the Son he loves (Colossians 1:13). That is surely the happy ending we want for our children. When we talk to our children about consequences we can also talk about grace.

### 4. A time for praise

Asaph's new perspective and discovery of God's amazing grace elicits from him one of the most beautiful expressions of adoration in all of Scripture:

'Whom have I in heaven but you?

And there is nothing on earth that I desire besides you.
My flesh and my heart may fail,
but God is the strength of my heart and my portion forever.'

Psalm 73:25 & 26

God alone satisfies. That is how God made us. And the more we give ourselves to pursuing and knowing him the more delight we will find. We will enjoy him forever. That too is why we want our children to trust Christ. The greatest pleasure known to man is knowing Christ.

Many hymnwriters have attempted to capture Asaph's rapturous sentiments. William Gadsby did it best.

Immortal honours rest on Jesus' head;
My God my portion and my living bread;
In him I live, upon him cast my care;
He saves from death, destruction and despair.

He is my refuge in each deep distress;
The Lord my strength and glorious righteousness;
Through floods and flames he leads me safely on,
And daily makes his sovereign goodness known.

My every need he richly will supply;
Nor will his mercy ever let me die;
In him there dwells a treasure all divine,
And matchless grace has made that treasure mine.

O that my soul could love and praise him more,
His beauties trace, his majesty adore;

Live near his heart, upon his bosom lean;
Obey his voice and all his will esteem.

## Praying with an eternal perspective

We do not know whether Job prayed for his children's health, safety and prosperity. In view of later events a cynic might say that perhaps he should have. What we do know is that this blameless and upright man was most concerned for his children's *spiritual* state (Job 1:5). Given the fact that none of them lived to old age, I would say that his priorities were right.

Jesus came to undo the devil's work and his miracles speak of that. He came to bring sight to the blind and life to the dead. Our children need their eyes opened; they are sick with the disease of sin; they are spiritually dead. Many different parents applied to Jesus on behalf of their children (Mark 7:24–30; John 4:43–54; Mark 5:36). Jesus graciously acceded to their requests.

There was, however, one occasion of request denied. We should learn from it. The mother of James and John came to ask a privileged position for her boys in Christ's kingdom (Matthew 19:20–21). She wanted them to have status. Jesus loved James and John too much to say yes to that one. Their request was an ignorant one, of course, in all sorts of respects, but it reminds us that our prayers as loving parents can be misdirected. When our desires and priorities are out of tune with God's, we may wonder at God's silence. James has some strong words:

'You ask and do not receive, because you ask wrongly, to spend it on your passions. You adulterous people! Do you not know that friendship with the world is enmity with God?'          James 4:3–4

We might pray for our children to succeed, but maybe within the eternal perspective in mind it might be more fruitful sometimes for our children to fail. Is that a harsh thing to say? Just read the Beatitudes in Matthew 5:3–12. Here is a description of the blessed life. Do we want our children to have a place at a top university or a place in the kingdom of heaven? Do we want them to get a good salary or do we want them to inherit the earth? Do we want them to see the world or to see God? Do we want them to be satisfied with marriage and family or to be satisfied in God?

Does it have to be either/or? You might wonder if they could perhaps have both, (and perhaps they will in God's providence) but as soon as you say that you have revealed that you haven't taken on board the eternal significance of those spiritual blessings. There is really no comparison between the house in Mayfair and the mansion in glory.

It may take a downturn in your child's life to bring him to Christ and the narrow way. You could pray that God would solve the immediate problem or you could pray that God would use this mess to drive him to Christ. A mother prayed for her wayward son who got into bad company and bad ways. His life spiralled downwards: a child whose mother he abandoned, drugs, theft, arrest, court, prison, release, re-arrest, another stretch of prison. His mother, grandmother and sister did not stop praying. At each stage they prayed. Perhaps they prayed that he would keep away from bad company; perhaps they prayed he would not get arrested; perhaps they prayed for a lenient judge. To all of those requests the answer was no. But they also prayed for his eternal soul. In his prison cell the young man started to read his Bible and he met Jesus. He was baptised in prison.

None of us want awful things to happen to our children and we rightly pray 'lead them not into temptation and deliver them from evil.' Mostly the things that happen are not as ghastly or serious as the experiences of the boy described above. And none of them are as bad as eternal damnation. But better the bad thing which puts them on the road to heaven than a heap of good stuff which might lead them to think that this life is just fine and dandy, thank you. And eternity fades into insignificance.

So perhaps we should pray some harder prayers for our children. Perhaps we should pray for the kind of ride which will bring them greatness of character. Perhaps we should pray that their self-confidence be dented so that they learn to lean on God more and find in him their strength and their portion, even if that means that some of their hopes and dreams, and ours, have to come crashing down.

When life is through, whose smile will count? Whose 'well done' do we hope will meet our children's astonished ears? (Matthew 25:21)

'And the angel said to me, "Write this: Blessed are those who are invited to the marriage supper of the Lamb." And he said to me, "These are the true words of God."'                                    Revelation 19:9

## For further reading:
'Forever' by Paul David Tripp (Zondervan)

# Conclusion

## 'I can't do this.'

*'Speak less to your kids and more to God. It is actually quite relaxing'*
From 'A Praying Life' by Paul E. Miller

When I was a teenager everybody tried to play a guitar, more or less. Sitting in other people's front rooms with friends on a similar journey, I worked at contorting the fingers of my left hand into impossible chord shapes. It was a long process which involved a lot of mindless strumming and picking and which resulted in some blistered fingers. The accepted text of the time was Bert Weedon's 'Play in a Day'. I and probably thousands of others can testify that Bert was optimistic. I never met anyone who played in a day. It just isn't that easy. Most of us found our own way through to our own level of mediocrity. But was not in a day, or days or even weeks.

There is no Bert Weedon equivalent in parenting and if there were I would maintain with some confidence that it would not work. As parents, we long for the cure-all technique, the short-cut to well-behaved, well-adjusted, bright and shiny children. That is why we are prey to any new-parenting idea that finds a column-inch in our newspapers.

New parents are inundated with advice. Pregnancy, childbirth and the care of infants is each beset by an avalanche of leaflets and books containing prescriptive and restrictive instructions. The sheer quantity and intensity of these can be quite intimidating. Of course there is much that is helpful and practical but, since every child is different, the advice is unlikely to meet every case. And 'all that stuff coming at you' can rob a parent of the confidence to just exercise intuition and common sense.

The main thrust of this book has been to encourage parents to be parents as God intended and as he himself has modelled: confident in their authority, consistent in their values, clear in their boundaries and loving in their relationships with their children. If all that seems obvious to the reader then I am glad to have reinforced what you are already doing. You may call it common sense. I observe that it is not as common as it ought to be.

Year on year secularism advances. It is a tide which, unless God shakes and moves in our nation again, is continually advancing, sometimes by stealth, frequently via popular media and recently through government legislation. I have tried to make the reader aware of some of the insidious as well as the obvious ways that this is happening. In doing so I am not blaming parents—we are all products of our time and many of the accepted mantras of child-rearing are in the air we breathe. But it does no harm to question popular assumptions and measure them against the standard of God's infallible word. It is indeed our duty to do so. Hear Paul in 2 Timothy 3:

> 'But understand this, that in the last days there will come times of difficulty. For people will be lovers of self, lovers of money, proud, arrogant, abusive, disobedient to their parents, ungrateful, unholy, heartless, unappeasable, slanderous, without self-control, brutal, not loving good, treacherous, reckless, swollen with conceit, lovers of pleasure rather than lovers of God ...'            2 Timothy 3:1–4

Paul's injunction to Timothy at the end of that paragraph is to have nothing to do with them. He is to be discerning. And so are we, as surely we recognise the above as a pretty accurate description of 21st century Britain. Paul then goes on to warn Timothy about how this teaching worms its way into people's home and gains control over weak-willed women (v. 6). Need I say more? With the world-wide web and every possible kind of media continually invading our senses the worming-in is going like the clappers. What is the answer to it?

In the remainder of the chapter Paul reminds Timothy that Scripture is to be his only guide. Certainly he might get stick for it (v. 12) but he must not give up.

> 'All Scripture is breathed out by God and profitable for teaching,

for reproof, for correction, and for training in righteousness, that the man of God may be complete, equipped for every good work.'

2 Timothy 3:16–17

Every good work includes the bringing up of children (1 Timothy 5:16). The Bible equips parents for this work. I plead with Christians not to allow passing psychological fads to displace its clear teaching.

## Simple but not easy

I believe that the Bible's clarity on the fundamentals brings simplicity, liberty and joy to raising children. That has been my experience. But that is not to say that I always found it easy. I hereby put it on record that in my thirty years of parenting I had frequent occasions of stress, failure and exhaustion. But I have learned through this and other God-given assignments of my life that on the day you review your performance with tears, shame and an overwhelming sense of inadequacy, you have come to a good place. The shambles of family life is there to teach parents that they need God. Paul Miller writes in his book 'A Praying Life':

> 'Mature Christians are keenly aware that they can't raise their kids. It's a no-brainer. Even if they are perfect parents, they still can't get inside their kids' hearts. That's why strong Christians pray more'.

## Commit them to God

Children really are all different. Every one. That is why techniques are doomed to failure. There are too many factors in the case.

A frustrated parent observed to me, 'I know every child is

unique, but mine is unique in a unique kind of way.' Parenting at that point was a hard road. Nobody understood. Stop. Someone does. The God who knit your child together in the womb knows and cares. Talk to him about it all.

Some readers of this book may have a child who is disabled, or sick, or on some kind of spectrum. God understands them all. Some children hardly sleep; some are incorrigibly wilful and stubborn; some are scarily bold; some are disappointingly wimpish. No parenting issue is too large or small, too weird, embarrassing or mundane to bring to the Father God. It is prayer that makes the difference as God works from the inside while you do your faltering best to follow his directions from the outside. This might be a prayer of years and in that time God will work on everyone in the case for their good, not least on the person who is praying.

The biggest mistake we can make in parenting is to think we have everything sorted. Speak less to your kids and more to God. He is a better parent than you or me.

To him alone be glory.